A View of The Future of Work

Charles Grantham, Norma Owen and Terry Musch

This book first took form as a compilation of white papers and blogs prepared by the FutureWork>ing<TOGETHER team for the Future of Work conference in San Luis Obispo in January 2012.

It has now developed a more sophisticated form, with the addition of significant new material. Each chapter is organized around a central question, and each question relates to issues of self-development and/or organizational development in context of a decade unfolding before all of us with exponential change. In a sense this treatment is the strategic work plan for the FutureWork>ing<TOGETHER tribe.

Join our tribe as we continue to explore new avenues of connection such as our Radio blog series. There is, of course, a website under construction, along with several blogs, Facebook accounts, and Twitter feeds.

http://www.blogtalkradio.com/fwt-guild

fwt@futureworkingtogether.com

Copyright Notice

© 2012 by Charles E Grantham, Norma A. M. Owen, and Terry L. Musch   All rights reserved. This book or any portion thereof may not be reproduced or used in any manner whatsoever without the express written permission of the publisher except for the use of brief quotations in a book review.

For those who purchase this manuscript in e-book form, the authors have provided this publication for your personal use only. You may not print or post this e-book, or make this e-book publicly available in any way. You may not copy, reproduce or upload this e-book, other than to read it on one of your personal devices.

First Printing, 2012

627 W. Lee Blvd
Prescott, AZ 86303

Plan of the Book

The table below is the roadmap for this book. On it we've plotted routes to the key questions explored in each chapter, to the organizing themes within the chapters, and to the type of "energy" that is the focus of each question.

Chapter	Question Answered	Theme[1]	Energy Realized
0-Backstory	Where did this come from?	Conception and birth of the idea	Shaping in-flowing energy
1-Drivers of change	What is manifesting?	Potentiality	Physical
2-Purpose	What is your purpose?	Giving and Receiving	Emotional
3- New Skills	What will be required?	Karma "cause and effect"	Ego
4- Artisans of Thought	What does it look like?	Minimal Effort	Social
5-New Workplace	How is it done?	Intention	Creativity
6-New Community	How is it perceived or seen?	Detachment	Intuition
7-Doing, Being and Living	How is it to be understood?	Dharma "Purpose in life"	Understanding

8-Thriving and Sustaining	What is the conscious connection?	Expanding beyond current limits	Transformation
9-Epilogue	What if…?	A look into the future scope	The unbroken circle
Resources	How to find a teacher?	Moving to the next level	Completing the pattern

These routes appear to be simple, linear, and logical. However, as you've probably guessed by now, we don't think in straight lines and neither does the future. Moreover, we are targeting three distinct audiences here that don't yet realize the extent to which they're connected. By the time you finish reading this, however, we feel confident that you will totally understand the nature of the connections and the logic of the inter-relationships. For those of you new to this type of thinking, check out the next page. The ForeSight Galaxy is a logic map; it will guide you through the material with maximum efficiency. Of course, we hope you go back and trace the other paths to develop an understanding of those relationships too. Above all, enjoy!

No matter your background or goals, everyone should start by reading chapters 0 and 1. Then, you can branch off, depending on your natural motivation. Public Sector-oriented folks may read Chapters 5, 6 and 8 before closing with the Epilogue. If you are more interested in the "personal" content, you may prefer to start with Chapters 2, 4 and 7 before looping back to the beginning. The private sector oriented readership (business folk) may jump ahead to Chapter 3 and then, just like the public sector oriented folks, close with the Epilogue. We hope alternatives like these will give you quick access to critical material, and then point you to connections you might not have considered when you started.

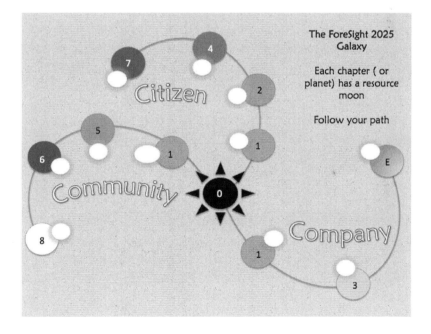

The symbols depicting each chapter may at first seem random, but each represents the core idea of its chapter. At the end of the book, we'll reveal the secret to the underlying pattern of the chapters, but why not see if you can figure it out first.

Contents

 ## Backstory   xiii

Chapter 0 tells the story of how this book came to be written. It speaks of our deep motivations. As a foundation for everything that follows, it also presents an integrated perspective of the forces shaping the future of work: culture, management focus, communication technology, and physical workspace design.

 ## Drivers of Change   2

Chapter 1 begins a deep dive into the ocean of change, beginning with an attempt to answer simple questions like: "what is happening," or "what is coming into being?" You could also say that this chapter focuses on the physical, tangible things that obscure a vision of the future. It also touches on the root causes of change—demographics, technology, and uncertainty—and describes how those drivers of change mediate the conflict between recent history and emerging purpose.

 ## Purpose: Compass & Gyroscope 23

The basic question posed in Chapter 2 is: "What is your purpose?" Chapter Two, is about being and emotions. It is intended to help readers become more aware, and to help welcome those persons who lived in the old reality into the new reality of the future. It also touches on self-gratification and its role in revealing our true core. Toward that end, the chapter lists key questions to ask, the principal fears we must overcome, and a suggested, development process for that revelation.

The New Skills: Leadership for the 21ˢᵗ Century   40

Chapter 3 focuses on 12 new leadership skills for the 21ˢᵗ Century, and makes the inarguable point that the skills that worked for us in the industrial era do not work today. This is a conceptual world, not a mechanized world. As a result, new leadership skills are needed in our global, hyper-connected world. The skills and competencies that are needed are knowable, and can be taught and understood intellectually. However, for a leader to stay the course and lead through change and adversity, this kind of self-esteem and self-leadership can only be developed through experience. This isn't rocket science. Tried and true principles of social psychology can help prepare our future leaders. And this psychology is valid across cultures in today's global business environment.

Artisans of Thought   55

Chapter 4 introduces what we call Artisans of Thought—that is, the next generation of human beings who will create economic and social value in our global society. Their story unfolds as a series of answers to the following questions: Who are they are, what do they do, how are they unique, how do they organize themselves, and how do they act upon the world. This chapter is intended for both the Artisans themselves, and for those who understand their importance in meeting the needs of our new society. Pick and choose what is important to you, but read the whole story.

The New Workplace   71

The central question in Chapter 5 is "How will work be done?" Much of the "how" it turns out depends on the "where," because changes in technology have now distributed the flow of work in time and space. The good news is that you can work anywhere, anytime. The bad news is that you can work anywhere, anytime. However, we are human "beings," not human "doings," therefore, in addition to a workplace we need a COLLABORATIVE PLACE to be comfortable, relaxed, and yet focused. Therefore, in the future we will gravitate to places where the intent may not be to work, per se, but to unleash our creativity. It is our belief that these forces will culminate in working closer to where we live, or where we normally congregate—in short, in our communities, not in some far-off office tower. An example of an emerging physical space where entrepreneurs and intrepreneurs can come together to collaborate is a Business Community Center^{SM} (BCC). The BCC is w here creative innovation will find a welcoming place in our communities, a center where we can both think broadly, and maintain focus.

The New Community   85

By Chapter 6 we will have moved from the question of "what is happening," to "what skills do I need," and on to "what will it look like?" That central question can be answered only through self-reflection, intuition, and imagination. Moreover, this answer will bear on the form of social organization, to nurture and support this emerging Artisan described in chapters 2 through 5. We suggest that the emergent social form is actually a back-to-the-future scenario; in this chapter, we will trace the history of guilds and the modern forces driving their re-emergence. We will also consider the failure of industrial institutions, technology that speeds up learning, a search for intimate community, and the devolution of power from the central state. Furthermore, we will discuss the need for social change along with a prescription of the functions new guilds might perform, and those they cannot.

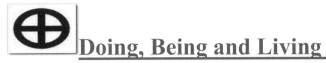
Doing, Being and Living   98

The basic question posed in Chapter 7 is: "How can we understand what needs to be done?" This chapter is about integrating who we are, what we do, and how we will "live." In short, it is about connecting with something larger than ourselves. Chapter 2, you may remember, was about our individual purpose, while this chapter brings readers to the end of the path, and deals with connecting and integrating that purpose with something at a higher, collective level. We call it a Talent Integration Ecosystem^{SM}

Thriving and Sustaining   113

Chapter 8 should not be considered the end of our short journey of discovery, but the beginning. The central question of this chapter is: "What is the conscious connection between a person, their community, and their work?" Therefore, this chapter is about YOUR transformation within your community, and the way a true understanding of that transformation will alter not only your career, and your life, but also the lives of those around you.

In order to thrive (not just survive) in the future you need to first get on firm ground. Remember back in Chapter 2 we talked about finding your purpose? Well that is all well and good, but as we wrote above, that initial dive was relatively shallow. Our good friend Terry has developed an approach intended to make us all more agile at the personal level. The 9E™ process; it is evolutionary and transformational in nature, and we hope it will inspire you to begin a journey that will continue for the rest of your life. Through a facilitated and structured process that raises your awareness of what you already know, you will become more satisfied with, engaged in, and fulfilled by the life you choose to live.

Epilogue   125

No collection of ideas concerning the future would be complete without a peek into the void beyond the present. So, here in our humble opinion are a few tantalizing thoughts about what we think is going to happen in the next few years.

This section is a re-print and update from an earlier document published by the Work Design Collaborative in 2005. Of the 28 predictions, we made then, 11 have come true by 2010. That's a 40% hit rate. Of the remainder, a number of them relate to structural changes in laws and regulations, which inherently lag significantly behind actual changes in social attitudes and behavior. We submit 17 of them for your consideration.

The Meanings of the Symbols   134

We're sure you have noticed that we like to use symbols. There are a couple of reasons for that. First, we are becoming an increasing symbolic world and we need to learn how to think symbolically. An art our ancestors were masterful at, but something we seem to have lost with becoming "civilized". Second, symbols connect us with a higher state of consciousness if you will.

The symbols we use come from two primary sources; Ancient Native American Indian religions and more contemporary Eastern traditions. It really reflects Charliepedia's Native heritage (25% Cherokee) and his recent study and practice of Rekei Master/Teacher.

We kick off each chapter with a symbol and the essence of its meaning. When viewing the future of work, we see a world that thrives in whole brain thinking. The introduction of the symbols at the beginning of each chapter lends focus, a wish for each reader and gives your right brain something to chew on while your left brain in busy with the text. If you're curious or just want to view the symbols and meanings in their entirety, we've listed them in the resource section at the end of the book.

Backstory – Where did this come from?

Symbol for a blending of triple realms. Blending of the three authors thoughts. Technically called a "triskele". Ancient Celtic in origin. Sometimes seen as the trinity. For us a bringing together of will, being and function.

Chapter 0 - The Backstory

"The quest for certainty blocks the search for meaning. Uncertainty is the very condition that impels us to unfold our powers."

Erich Fromm

How Did We Get Here?

This book has a long, sordid history. The short of it however, is that Terry Musch, Norma Owen and I got together in late 2010 and hatched an idea about helping communities move into the 21st Century. You would think that three relatively mature and educated adults would have known better. But no, we launched into an uncertain world with an untested idea buoyed only with the unbridled energy of a new puppy.

What started out to be another conference on "the future of work" morphed into an Unconference, a new community and the birth of a brand we call FutureWork>ing<TOGETHER. We dabbled in technology, websites, twitter accounts and Facebook pages. We produced a lot of material and generally made ourselves state-of-the-practice experts in the emerging workplace. And as with most futurists it is often difficult to understand why people don't understand the convergence of accelerating forces of change.

So, here we are over a year later with negative cash flow, a bunch of new great friends and the beginnings of a virt-real community dedicated to the cause of helping others create a community framework able to adapt, integrate and thrive during dramatic shifts of change- economic, climate and/or technological. This book is our attempt at pulling together most of the material we created into a coherent whole. *The gospel according to T, Norms and Charliepedia.*

A Cautionary Note for Right Brain Readers

Visualize a double strand of human DNA. It is composed of various molecules in specific sequences; its strands twist around one another and it's folded over and over. That's how this book is put together. You will see specific molecules mentioned time and time again, but not always in the same sequence. Strands of major thought (like community, guilds, leadership and evolutionary development) will wind together and fold over one another. If you are looking for a finely tuned, linear, logical argument, please stop reading right now. You will be frustrated, upset and probably use this tome as kindling.

If, on the other hand, you are seeking a roadmap of the 21st Century workplace and what it will take to be successful in that place, then you have arrived and welcome to our "future is here now" world. One hint, there is a plan, an overarching cognitive structure to this book. We'll see if you can figure out the mystery. We reveal it at the conclusion should the mystery still elude you and if you enjoy Dan Brown novels, you will find this interesting.

But let's start with some background—backstory in newspeak. The first part of this chapter is about the bigger, larger, 50,000-foot image of what is happening on our world. It's important to know where you are on this map and then where you want to go. A successful journey begins with a map. But the map is not the territory. Unpredictable things will happen on the journey and there will be bumps in the road. Buckle up, take a deep breath and let's begin.

Concordance and Re-FORMation of the Workplace

More organizations are moving towards a community model in their structure. A community model allows them to interact more closely with each other, to be creative and to get products to market quicker. But for communities to be truly effective, and not dysfunctional, they need to align their form, focus and work processes. In a more traditional organization with a maximum of face-to-face communication, a lot of mis-alignments could be tolerated because there was so much redundancy in communication. But in a virtual world (aka community) redundancy is restricted. You have to get the right message to the right person at the right time. There is far less room for error and customers are less tolerant of errors because they can go elsewhere with less cost.

Particular forms of communication patterns and shifts in management attention support community development and sustainability. The important shift is that there is a physical manifestation of community operations. One of the greatest challenges we face in moving towards a highly technological, global and for purposes of discussion the Internet economy is to find a way to bring these cultural, process, form and architectural dimensions into concordance. If these dimensions are in concordance then there is a maximum of potential being realized in the community. If not, the community will seem to be out of touch with its customers, slow and in-efficient.

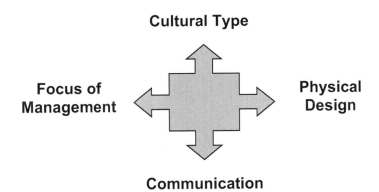

There are several perspectives in the recent business press that talk to each of these points. Our aim here is to bring these perspectives together and give you a set of guidelines for constructing your own effective community of commerce.

Dimensions of culture

"Culture, in a word, is community." This quote from Rob Goffee and Gareth Jones in the Harvard Business Review begins their analysis of different types of cultures or communities they say are the glue that holds modern companies together. They contend that different types of cultures are more or less effective in certain business environments. Furthermore, they contend that leaders need to first understand their environment, and then construct a culture that supports that type of environment. They describe two basic dimensions to their map of communities.

Sociability is "a measure of sincere friendliness among members of a community" and **Solidarity** is "a measure of a community's ability to pursue shared objectives quickly and effectively." These two dimensions construct a grid, which defines the four major types of communities.

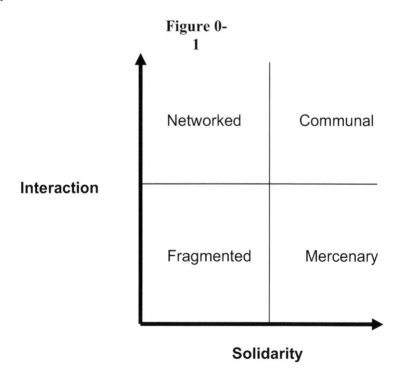

Figure 0-1

Networked organizations are known "not by a lack of hierarchy but by a perfusion of ways to get around it." They are all very friendly with one another but operate on different business agendas. Usually you see this in a company with multiple operating divisions that is only unified by 'the way we do things around here." These cultures are consummate political atmospheres where managers spend a great deal of time forwarding personal agendas.

Networked organizations can be very effective in business environments where there are long strategic time frames spanning years if not decades, the ability to operate inside local cultures is required, and where the corporate headquarters can do well with little inter-divisional coordination. Today, a great example of this type of organization is Hewlett-Packard with its many divisions, business segments and its emphasis on the "H-P Way." However, as we have seen over the past few months, the "H-P Way" may be changing in response to an evolving business environment where time frames are shorter, local customs' have given way to global e-commerce, and corporate success depends on unity.

Fragmented organizations are ugly places to work. Any sense of belonging and function is subverted for economic gain. People don't identify themselves as 'members' but rather as 'employees.' "People work with their doors shut or at home". Process based organizations, for example many manufacturing organizations that outsource large parts of the work, are effective fragmented organizations. Professional organizations, such as university environments, can also work well in this type of culture. Goffee and Jones also suggest that 'fragmented cultures often accompany organizations that have become virtual…"

Mercenary organizations are your classical start up firm. With total unity their purpose is to "defeat the competition." They respond quickly and are united in their effort. Work and social life are clearly separated thus allowing an intolerance of poor performance. The emphasis is on performance, performance, performance. They will execute the plan, change on a dime and throw you out in a flash. Little loyalty exists.

Mercenary cultures work well when change in markets and products is very rapid, economies of scale can be reached, and goals are specific and measurable. Software giants like Microsoft personify the mercenary organization.

Finally, **communal organizations** are characterized by an emphasis on social affairs as well as business performance. Unfortunately, this dual emphasis between focus, or solidarity, and interaction can create an oscillating tension and consume time. Some people think this form of organization is inherently unstable. However, we do not agree that this is necessarily true in a Communities of Commerce environment.

Communal type organizations are especially effective when teamwork across extended boundaries is required, learning synergies exist among its members, and there is a clear long-term development strategy. In a "Communities of Commerce" environment, the inherent tension can be resolved by moving around organizational forms as required and by not getting the entire firm stuck in one cultural mode. Multi-mode operation may be the ultimate strength of the virtual environment- because of its inherent fluidity.

Communication Patterns

Henry Mintzberg and his colleagues believe there are four basic patterns to communication in organizations. While, they don't see these patterns as varying along any particular dimension, we believe a deeper analysis of social network structure in business firms show these differences are distributed in terms of their network dimensions.[2]

Using our familiar 2X2 matrix, we see patterns of communication in this way. Density of communication refers to the amount of 'interconnectedness' in community member communications. Few interconnections represent low density. Channels refer to the absolute number of ways to communicate something ranging from a single step-by-step channel to a multi-channel capacity.

Figure 0-2

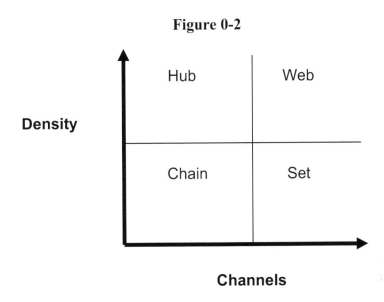

Hub type communications occur when several signals come into and move outward from a single point. It looks like a hub and spoke system that is familiar to the airline model. Hub models can handle quite a bit of traffic, say from several operating divisions; but sometimes the hub becomes congested and everything backs up. When communications get congested, overall traffic slows down until congestion is cleared. Federal Express is an example of the Hub Model in the distribution environment.

In the **Chain** communication model, communications flow through one single channel and that channel is not connected to any other source. This model represents strict hierarchical communication in serial form. From President to VP to Director and on down. Upward communication works in the same way. The Chain communication model tends to be slow, it offers significant distortion to the signals, and it is not error correcting.

Set communications are low bandwidth, disconnected parallel patterns. The same signal goes out several pathways simultaneously. These are independent elements following the same general rules. Examples of Set communications include academic departments, lawyers in a law firm and similar environments.

Web communication is the most complex offering multiple signals over multiple paths at the same time without any apparent central control. This is how the Internet is designed at its core. Packets of information (messages) move over multiple routes, error correct themselves through redundancy and are tremendously robust to the failure of any one link.

Management Focus

We have talked about the relationship of complexity and communication as two dimensions that underlie differences in management focus of attention. If you go back to that diagram and move the complexity and creativity axes, it bears a closer resemblance to the two perspectives we have just outlined. The matrix now looks like:

Figure 0-3

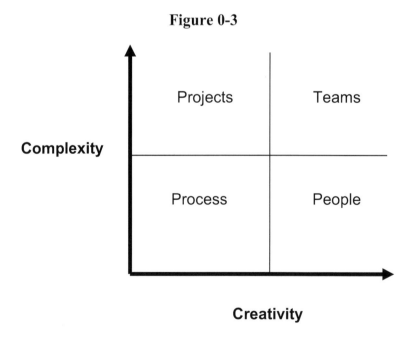

Just to recap. If high complexity and low creativity is your typical project management environment, it has set procedures that must be executed with a high degree of interdependency. An example of this environment is Federal Express where timing of everything coming into the hub is of paramount importance; but each delivery is within itself a rather routine affair. Low creativity and low complexity is where management focuses its' attention on getting the process right, eliminating waste in execution, and following a rigid set of procedures. Examples include call centers that have scripts for customer problem resolution. Environments of high creativity and low complexity are the relative isolation of deep domain experts working various parts of a larger project; such as technical writers, lawyers and professors. Teams based environments are both high on creativity and complexity and they have a flavor of true collaboration. Team members create on the fly and interaction is often very intense and complex.

Spatial Organization

The last way of looking at communities is to look at how they organize themselves in time and space. This is the province of architecture. But architecture now has to look at organizing human activity in both a physical and virtual environment. Frank Duffy, a noted European architect, is a pioneer in this field.

Duffy organizes space (both real and virtual) around two dimensions - "interaction" and "autonomy". Interaction for Duffy moves from individuals to teams--roughly a measure of amount of interaction. Autonomy varies from procedural activities (with low tolerance for variation) to knowledge based activities where value is added in the act of creation of new knowledge.

Figure 0-4

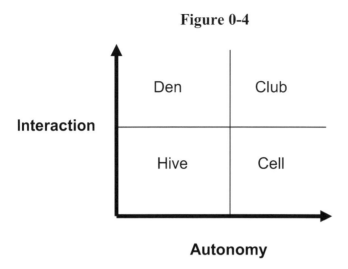

Duffy's spatial metaphors evoke some strong images; as they are intended to do. But they also bring to mind pictures of how communities work together. Dens look like your typical low rise support areas in modern corporations. Semi-private areas are places where a lot of activity takes place in repetitious processes with functions like administrative support teams.

Hives on the other hand are the ultimate in "Dilbertvilles" as they have come to be called. Cube farms are places where individuals conduct endless processes, a step at a time. Any back office processing operations resembles cube farms. They are designed for maximum cost efficiency and they do not foster, in fact they often impede, interaction among community members.

Cells look like your private corner office or the monk's cell in which members' labor in highly individual activities. Cells are designed to be personal spaces with barriers to intrusion. The artists' loft is another example. Finally, the Club looks like a highly re-configurable area that provides both public and private space. The Club is used according to the task at hand--be it public celebration or private chat.

Putting the Pieces Together

In our opinion, there is uniformity, which underlies the various dimensions used by these authors. They are:

Interaction: The ability to continually be connected and related to community members and customers. This corresponds to Goffee and Jones' sociability; Mintzberg's density; our idea of complexity and Duffy's own definition of interaction. It's about the pattern of interactions among the community. They move from fragmented serial, process based interactions to interactions that are friendly, dense, and circle around an object, idea or particular piece of work activity.

Freedom: Continuous conception and implementation of new ideas that provide added value for customers. Goffee and Jones called this 'solidarity;' Mitzberg described multiple channels of communication; we see this vector as creativity and Frank Duffy calls it "autonomy." This dimension is innovation--the process that creates new products for new markets. It goes from routine, pre-defined processes to creative application of ideas to novel situations.

Figure 0-5

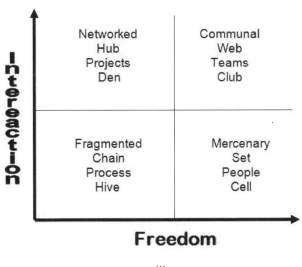

Now we have a picture of the various elements that must be brought into concordance for the effective development of communities of commerce. This integrated framework is what has been missing in all the cases we spoke about earlier. In our case studies, we find that effective communities integrated these four elements.

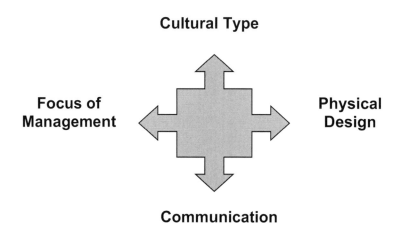

We believe we are moving away from a predominantly fragmented organization culture (and community) with chained communication and management emphasis on process and a hive structure to a more communal model (aka communities of commerce) with networks of communication and an emphasis on teams and multi-functional structures in space and time.

There is a brief self-assessment questionnaire in the resources chapter that will help you locate where your organization (or community) is located in this framework. This concludes our assessment of the structural changes we are experiencing and most likely with more technical information and background than you cared to know. Bottom line, the trend revealing itself is that we are becoming more communal, network based, team organized and "clubby." In the following chapters, we will take a deep dive into these factors.

Into the Breach

Something's happening here. What it is, ain't exactly clear.
- Buffalo Springfield

We have rapidly been moving to a more distributed work and lifestyle model. The events of September 11, 2001 and the following weeks focused a number of converging social and psychological factors that had been unfolding for five years.[3] The very social fabric of relationships between employees and employers was forever changed. It appeared the war for talent was over and that talent won! Now what?

We foresee a massive physical re-distribution of talent in the United States, if not the world, spurred on by the Internet technology and driven by the workers' intense desire for both safety and a higher quality of life. When this happens, people are drawn to places where they feel a sense of community and common purpose. Historically, libraries played a role in providing a 'place' for people to gather and gain access to knowledge, information and, yes, ultimately each other. Now we will look at how centers of information, tools and social networks (i.e., libraries) can serve a role in the unfolding future of work.

Shift Has Happened – A New Focus for Society

We believe the economy today is in the early stages of an unprecedented shift in what people perceive to be important and how value for them is created. Not only has talent replaced land, capital and raw materials as the source of economic value, but the values, goals and expectations of talent have also shifted. Future success in business will depend directly on the ability to understand these shifts and to redesign workforce environments and workplace strategies accordingly.

Recently many companies have faced the hard lesson that what goes up (i.e., demand, revenue, profitability, headcount and floor space) all too often comes back down – and often at warp speed. Downsizing, restructuring, refinancing, divesting and refocusing are difficult and painful for both business and the displaced human capital. Yet all too often these efforts have produced little more than "do more with less;" reducing the workforce without reducing the work, delaying essential investments, subleasing unused space, cutting travel, eliminating training and development, even shrinking marketing and R&D budgets. While these tactics may help ensure short-term survival, they generally do so at the cost of weakening long-term viability.

Successful organizations focus on minimizing workforce support costs (i.e., technology, facilities, compensation and benefits, travel, development and management). At the same time, they must ensure that critical workers have access to the information and communications capabilities that are needed in order to be highly efficient at all times and *in all locations* -- the office, home and community center. Organizations that are in it for the long haul creates working environments that attract and leverage highly motivated, high-performing knowledge workers.

Today's knowledge workers are not just looking for jobs or for income, but for opportunities to contribute *and* to maintain their preferred lifestyle – to make a meaningful difference in a meaningful way. They want to achieve a new kind of balance in their lives – a balance between work and play, work and family, and work and personal growth. For high-performing talent today, lifestyle has become just as important as work style; in many respects, the two have become inseparable. September 11th 2001 and then the financial meltdown of 2007-2009 brought clarity to this point and many workers are re-examining and recommitting to their personal priorities.

To further complicate matters, computing and communications technologies have transformed the traditional workplace into a virtual "work*space.*" The idea of working "any time, any place" has become a reality, with hundreds of variations on that theme. Knowledge work can be conducted from an office, from an airport lounge, on an airplane, in a car or at the local coffee shop. It often includes real-time communication and collaboration with colleagues located virtually anywhere on the planet. Whether it is telecommuting, remote work, mobile work, or – most likely – an ongoing and changing mix of all these forms, knowledge workers today have choices about where and when to work – and who to work with. Knowledge workers are exercising their myriad choices. The de-centralization of the workforce is well underway in the United States and globally and with it, the shift of power from the employer to the employee closely follows.

There is a quick check assessment of cultural type in the Resources section for this chapter. Try it to find out what kind of organization you're in.

Drivers of Change – What is pulling us into the future?

Symbol for change. African Adinkra symbol MMERE DANE originated from the Akan people in Ghana and represents the changes and dynamics of life. Many things occur beyond our direct control (or the illusion of control) this symbol reminds us to not resist these forces but blend with them.

Chapter 1 - Drivers of Change

This chapter answers the basic question of "what is happening" or "what is manifesting and coming into being"? You might say this chapter focuses on physical, tangible, concrete things that cloud the vision of the future. It's about the root causes or drivers of change that mediate the relationship between our history and our emergent purpose.

Demographics

Interim Technologies (now known as Spherion) conducted a longitudinal panel study of emerging workforce demographics since 2003. They identified a consistent trend towards a shift in the basic social psychology, or attitudes of workers. The major shift is in attitudes about job security, openness to workplace change, responsibility for one's career development, the definition of loyalty to one's employer, and the degree of stimulation and challenge desired at work. The following list outlines some of these basic differences in attitude between the generations. It should be noted that this issue is really about "Generational Flux;" it's more about attitude than age.

Traditional Employees	Emerging Employees
Demand long term job security	Reject job security as a driver of commitment
Believe employers are responsible for career growth	Take personal responsibility for career growth
Are less satisfied with their jobs	Are more satisfied with their jobs
Believe changing jobs often is bad for career growth	Believe frequent job changes are part of career growth
Define loyalty as tenure	Define loyalty as accomplishment
View work as an opportunity for income	View work as a chance to grow

Think of traditional employees as being older members of the workforce, who have therefore usually been in the workforce longer. Typically, these workers carry with them the values of the post-war, fifties culture. Emerging employees, on the other hand, come from the group often referred to as Generation X, the post-baby boom generation that began to enter the workforce in the late 1980s.

Quite clearly, we can see that there are some basic conflicts in the attitudes traditional and new employees bring to very basic things associated with jobs and work. Those of you who are part of the generation between traditional and emerging employees are members of the baby boom generation. You may well be feeling the tension between the traditional and emerging values the generations above and below you bring to work.

This problem is becoming even more acute as we see Millennials, those born after 1982; enter the workforce in significant numbers. Imagine the situation of an emerging employee who reports to a more traditional employee/manager. It's easy to see where many significant problems in communication, motivation, and compensation will arise. Or, if you're a manager in your early forties, consider the challenges you face if one of your key employees is in his/her late fifties and has a conflict with that bright young twenty-seven year old you just hired!

Here are some more key findings from the study[4]:

- 44% of traditional workers believe that <u>as an employer</u> they cannot offer long-term job security; therefore, there is no reason to go out of your way to help them succeed. Only 4% of emerging workers hold this view. This means that a new generation of managers will emerge within ten years that believe they have some responsibility to promote continuing education among those who work for them.

- 45% of traditional workers agree with the statement, "I don't like my job but it provides me with a paycheck," compared to only 2% of emerging workers.

- 81% of traditional workers believe that changing jobs every few years can be damaging to a person's career advancement, compared with only 30% of emerging workers.

- 87% of emerging workers believe employers are not responsible for an individual's career development. Only 51% of traditional workers agree.

- 97% of emerging workers believe loyalty today isn't about tenure, but about the contributions, a worker makes on the job. Only 69% of traditional employees agree.

- 98% of emerging workers agree that work provides them with a chance to grow. Only 70% of traditional workers agree.

So, we can see that the social psychology of the workplace is changing dramatically. We believe it is acutely important for us to be aware that these shifts are being driven by events far larger than ourselves and the dynamics of the particular companies we work for. They have as much to do with our period in history, the attitudes of the generations that came before us, and the emergence of new challenges that lay ahead of us, as with the unique dynamics of individual companies.

The Changing Face of Work

Our values and attitudes toward work aren't the only changes around us. Demographics are driving a fundamental change in how we work together. Consider that in the United States alone our workforce was 125 million in 1990 reached 151 million by 2005 and is projected to be 164 million by 2015[5]. Surprisingly, the 39 million increase represents a slowdown in growth of the labor force.

At the same time, as the rate of growth in the workforce is slowing, the overall number of jobs will increase. So, if we have an increase in the number of jobs and a slowdown in the growth of the labor pool, we can expect an increasing need to look outside the US for workers. As work becomes even more of a global issue profound political and social issues will continue to emerge. In the United States, there are special "H1 Visa's" for talented foreign nationals. However, the number of these visas is controlled by the US

Congress and fluctuates depending on the political mood in Washington DC.

As the workforce becomes more global, its ethnic makeup is also changing. White non-Hispanic men are becoming a smaller percentage of the male workforce, with their overall participation expected to fall from 79% in the 1990's to 73% by 2005 and 67% by 2012. Hispanic men and women saw the greatest increase in workforce participation, rising from 8% in the 1990's to slightly over 11% in 2005, a 45% increase. During the same period, women's participation in the workforce increased from 40% of the labor force in 1990's to 47% by 2005. The recession of 2006-2010 somewhat skewed the data, but we believe this trend will continue.

The workforce as a whole will also age with the median age increasing from about 36 years to slightly over 40 years of age. 15% of the labor pool will be older workers (over 55) by 2015, up from 12%. One conclusion you might reach from this is that studies of worker attitudes today tell us little about the values and attitudes that will dominate the workplace of the future.

The level of education required in this new workforce will also change. The fastest growing occupations are already those, which employ knowledge workers, where a college education is a minimum requirement. A picture of an older, more educated and higher paid workforce emerges. This workforce, with different attitudes and expectations about the relationship of people to their jobs, is a central driver of change as a component of the demographic shifts. Now we turn to the second driver: technology.

Technology

While social, individual, and generational changes are important drivers of the changes we are in today, technology is equally important. Technology has been affecting organizations for a long time, since the dawn of the printing press, and, more recently, with the explosion of inventions that ushered in the Industrial Revolution in the 19th Century. Thanks to the changes that occurred during those eras, we have had telephones in business for almost 100 years, computers for 40 years, and personal computers for 15 years. BYOD (Bring Your Own Device), the most recent trend in the last few years, is bringing a wider range of technological tools into the workplace and pushing organizations into technological change even faster.

In this book, the trend we focus on is the shift from mainframe computing —and the organizational structures and systems that flow from it — to the paradigm in which network computing become dominant. Additionally, in the not too distant future, biological Nano technology will further shift the structures, systems and tools as well as the role and sophistication of work. As a framework for studying this shift, we offer an overview of the role of computers and how they have impacted our relationship to work over the past fifty years.

From an historical perspective, the role of computers in our consciousness and in our lives has passed through five distinct stages with a sixth stage about to launch. Each stage has a distinct purpose, principal, and root metaphor.

Stage One: In the mid-1950s, we thought of computers as tools for solving scientific and engineering problems more quickly. To the computer scientists who cared for the massive arrays of vacuum tubes and steel, the principle governing their work was that the machine was preeminent.

The rest of working population, if they thought about computers at all, saw the application of computer power as almost mystical. The root metaphor to describe the role of computers at that time in society started with the back room; that is the place where the computer wizards practiced the mysterious art of engineering.

Stage Two: From the mid-1950s to about 1967, the purpose of computer use was to centralize business data resources. What had been mystical tools reserved for scientific research began to move into the more pragmatic world of work. Computers during this period routinized business operations, such as payrolls and invoice processing. Control became the principle as computer engineers search through the business and began centralizing processing power and strengthening middle management.

While Stage One of computer evolution had an almost mystical aura, the root metaphor during the 1960s was the data processing center: You dropped off your card deck, and returned the next morning to see if your program (the batch file) had run. You didn't exactly understand what it meant for the program to run. There was still a great gulf separating people who used computers at work and those who did not.

Stage Three: The period from about 1967 into the late 1970s was the frontier stage of computing characterized by an explosion of compute power. Everything, without question, was subject to automation. Computer professionals continued to be the keepers of the jealously guarded corporate database, but access to its mysteries started to open up.

Each business department had its own wizard who could talk to the keepers of the database, as the warehouse became the metaphor of the period. The department wizard would disappear into the hushed halls of the MIS department, reappearing with information and directions he could share with the rest of his group. That group was connected to the corporate database via the "dumb terminals" that sat on everyone's desk. However, the information the database contained was often as difficult to make sense of as it had been in the days of the computer-as-back-room.

Stage Four: As dumb terminals gave way to the local processing power of the desktop personal computer (PC), the 1980s became the decade of the neighborhood mechanic. Information resource centers sprang up all over the business with their own super-mini computers and localized databases. Technical specialties grew up, as control over the data moved from the center to the periphery.

Each manager had a local guru who had responsibility for departmental-level data. Instead of a single, massive warehouse, the root metaphors changed again and computing power came from the neighborhood garage, the local shop where people very much like the rest of us might discover the next great thing. Conducting business without access to computers became very difficult to visualize.

Stage Five: As a new the century dawns, we're in the fifth stage of the evolution of the relationship between worker and their computerized machines. In this stage, application tools let people tailor computer power to their needs. Computer professionals are seen as business team members, not wizards or arcane keepers of isolated warehouses. <u>Partnership</u> is the central image. Computer science, in the form of MIS and IS departments, often with sub-specialties like Finance or Human Resources, assists in designing core business processes to take advantage of technology's capabilities.

Stage Six: We anticipate that the next stage will see the further democratization of computers, as computing power moves from under the desk to the laptop. <u>Hunters and farmers</u> will become the dominant metaphors: Some people take the tools to the field; others stay home with them. Hunters carry their tools with them. They will be mobile enabled by peer-to-peer networks. Farmers leave them at a central location; where they return on a regular basis.

What's important to take from all this is the realization of how profoundly the role of computers has changed in our lifetime? If you are over forty, there's a good chance you can remember a time when information stored in computers was almost impossible for ordinary workers to have access to. If you are over thirty-five, you can probably remember an era in which laptop computers and cellular phones were not part of your toolbox at work.

If you are in your twenties, the idea of taking long paper punch cards to a mysterious basement room where a ghostly-pale clerk takes them from you to run through the computer's batch processing system at night probably sounds like something from the era of Dickens and Queen Victoria. But it was the norm less than twenty-five years ago.

Kinds of Technologies

The new technology of work is the intersection of four elements, not all of which you're probably accustomed to thinking of as "technology:"

- Education
- Computers
- Telecommunications, and
- Work

Two of these technologies, telecommunications and computer software, have been coming together for some time now. If you think about the latest cellular phones, which let you check your email from the airport, on the run, receive pages – in text or voice format – and even do something as prosaic as make a telephone call, you have to agree that it's almost impossible to distinguish where computers leave off and telecommunication systems begin.

On the other hand, you probably aren't used to thinking of education and work practices as technologies. But the emergence of multimedia, virtual reality and the Internet has done more than just add new tools to the same old stuff; they've transformed the nature of work and education themselves. Music TV programs now do news segments; classrooms employ videos with cartoons to illustrate points. We use technology to learn about technology (i.e., games to learn how to code), and technology gives us access to information we never could have discovered without it.

In other words, the interaction between the tools and data is itself integral to the technological advances we're making. Think of educational data as providing the **content** of the technology. Computers and software are the **form** of the technology, its general structure. In the context of the future of work, work practices are the **style** of the communication. Telecommunications are the **channel**.

Education is not often thought of as a technology. In our view education, or the process of learning and applying knowledge to business problems, is something that is becoming a fundamental part of the workplace. Traditionally we think of education as an activity that occurs while we're in the formal learning situations such as high school or college. Education is becoming more of an ongoing day-to-day activity in the new world of work. Education in this context teaches you not only new skills (which is really training) but education on values, ethics and totally new ways of thinking. Education in this context is an activity, which helps shape, and reshapes our basic values and attitudes towards work, our work mates and behavior in the workplace.

The education that you bring to your job is no longer sufficient for you to remain effective in that job as the job changes during the transition to the new world of work. The phenomenon of just in time education is partially precipitated by the Google search function. With a few keywords along with the words "how to" put into the Google engine, typically reveals multiple ways to learn at the moment of need in a way that best suits your learning style. We need to integrate educational activities very tightly with our telecommunications channels, the style of the communication (witness what Web browser design has done to the way we see computers), work content and forms of the technology.

We conducted a case study in Silicon Valley that examined over 20 high-tech firms and correlated the amount of money, in time; they spent on on-the-job education for their employees. We found that the most successful companies, in terms of increased revenue and profits, were those companies that spent on average 20 percent of their workers' time every week learning new things. That signifies a tremendous investment in education in the new workplace.

It's our contention that people and companies who are successful in this new world of work will be those that devote a significant amount of time and energy on educating themselves and their employees.

By changing one or more variables - content, form, style, and/or channel it is possible to alter the resulting whole that emerges from the interaction of the parts. These technologies are the ones we need to look at more closely to understand how they move from being just tools--to something that helps us stay connected. For example, take the Internet. Telecommunications (all those modems, phone lines, routers etc.) is the roadway, or **channel**, by which you move from different locations in cyberspace.

Computers and software, especially the "browser" governs how we see information on the Internet--it defines the **form**. When browsers first started out they provided a rich set of static graphics and changed the way we saw things on the Internet. It was a vast improvement over simple text. But now the **form** has evolved and we have dynamic graphics (i.e., moving images) sound and short video clips. Content is another matter. What we can access on the Internet is also changing rapidly. Sovereign laws of one country don't govern issues like censorship anymore; because the data (or content) is located on a server somewhere in cyberspace, and unless you can read Internet Protocol (IP) addresses, you don't know WHERE the information is coming from.

So, we need to look at how all four of these components of communication interact. Communicating on the Web is becoming an elevated art form much like movie making or other creative activities. Technology has been wrestled from the hands of its' inventors and is being turned over to everyone to use in their own unique way to connect to others with whom they want to interact.

Uncertainty[6]

> *"When you question the basic premise which you have worked under for the last 15 to 20 years, which is that markets are rational and efficient, there is a case for a different approach both to monetary policy and regulation."*[7]

Risk and uncertainty are two different things, which are often confused in people's minds. So let's start with definitions.

Risk: The potential that a given choice of action will have an undesirable outcome. Note that this definition implies that your choice of action can have an impact on the outcome. All actions in life carry a risk, albeit some more than others.

Uncertainty: Lack of knowledge of the possibility or impact of future events.

Backstory

As our social economy moves towards a global model and the interdependencies of systems (i.e., political, social, cultural and economic) increases, so does uncertainty. "Management" of uncertainty becomes nearly impossible; in the sense that's its' "management" would decrease the possibility of events that have an adverse impact on us. For example, you can't "manage" the weather or natural disasters such as catastrophic seismic occasions. Standing in the middle of an open field in a thunderstorm would be high risk because you (should) know there is a high probability of lightning strikes.

However, at the same time it becomes increasingly possible to "manage" risk. Our interconnectedness and speed of information flows makes the effects of all actions more visible and pronounced. In other words, you may correct a course of action quicker and minimize any adverse effects if you have in place sensing systems, which detect (and amplify) the signals of these impacts.

Case Study #1: TrashCo Inc. comes up with an idea that seems to fit between two market niches; however, no one has ever tried to bridge the gap between segments. Seems like the George Carlin School of marketing. Take two things that have never been stuck together before and stick them together, and people will buy it. But seriously, TrashCo was faced with a situation where they didn't even know what questions to ask prospective customers. Their solution to this uncertainty puzzle? They took the idea and actually involved potential customers in building the new product. What they got was a very rapid fail, improve, fail, and improve development cycle. The key here is that they took action and didn't get paralyzed by analysis in an unknown market.

Nice story, but what does that mean in everyday practice? Let me back up a bit and translate this story into something a bit more practical for the entrepreneur. Introducing a product into a market carries some risk. It may, or may not, be accepted. If it is accepted then sales increase; if it is not, then there are no sales. The risks can be managed in a number of ways. For example, market research and testing or rapid prototyping and testing.

However, this type of risk management only works in markets where knowledge of customer behavior is known. Innovative products or "game changing" business models fall into another category of uncertainty. And then the question changes. Let me give you an example. Imagine conducting a focus group among members of a lost African tribe. You work for Boeing and you want to know how wide you should make the seats in First Class on the next 787. There is no way you will get valuable product design data from this experiment because the product possibility you are presenting is so far away from the potential customers understanding, they really can't answer. You have entered the realm of uncertainty.

So, it is important to understand if you are dealing with a manageable, knowable "risk" or if you are dealing in the universe of "uncertainty".

Why is this important for entrepreneurs?

You have to know the game you are playing to make the right decisions. Do you know the rules, or are you in a new game? Usually the payoff is greater in new games rather than existing ones; so the value of your company depends on the game you are playing.

Case Study #2: Old Me, Inc. One frightening type of uncertainty is the personal kind. In this case, an individual contributor had to face up to the fact that the rules (or requirements of an old job) didn't change so much, as they went away. She found that everything that had spelled success for 20+ years didn't matter anymore. The classic case of being "over qualified". You leave a *job and find you can't get back into it because what you are good at isn't needed anymore. <u>Uncertainty of self</u>. How do you deal with that? In this case meeting the uncertainty came through a process of going back to overarching core skills. It's not enough to know how to use a wrench anymore, for example, but understanding the engineering principles of the machine to be maintained. Old Me, Inc. changed her brand identity to be more general, and less technical, and linked those competencies to needs of sales prospects. Results: back in the mix in 6 months and in more senior positions than before.*

This kind of story is incredibly important now because there is a high probability that our global economy is entering a new game phase where many of the "old rules" no longer apply uniformly. Risk (and it's management) doesn't go away; but the degree of uncertainty goes through the roof.

We are also seeing a corresponding shift in just how risk management, or planning occurs. Tales such as the JP Morgan $3B debacle in 2012 illustrates that "strategic planning" needs a paradigm also. We suggest the shift is moving from scenario planning to gaming and adaptive methodologies.

So, the question is: Are you in the old economy or the emerging one? You have a different set of action options given your answer to that key question. Defining your business model suddenly becomes a bit more complicated than a spreadsheet exercise.

One of the first questions you need to ask a budding entrepreneur is about their understanding of the market they are entering. What are the rules of behavior and how are you prepared to mitigate that risk of making the wrong choice? Obviously, I am a little nervous in today's high uncertainty environment about those who maintain they understand all the rules. Lack of humility equals stupidity.

Case Study #3: Spookytunes, LLC. This is the ultimate. The rules completely and permanently change. This case concerns a profession that grew up over a 50-year period and suddenly (OK over a year) everything Spookytunes did was made illegal by a shift in the regulatory environment. Something like this - "candy is a health threat and you can't sell it legally anymore." This is a step function shift in uncertainty. The old world has gone away and no new definitions of "proper" behavior are given. You just can't do that anymore. Psychologists will tell you that simply telling someone that "it is inappropriate behavior" is providing only minimal knowledge. You still don't know what to do. Resolution of uncertainty here? Liquidate the assets and re-invest in a different industry. Spookytunes reinvented itself into another entity focused on a very different market. The leverage came from using the old business network and reputation to find a high value in an emerging market.

What do you do?

The good news is that there are ways to manage risk and reduce uncertainty for new businesses. The need for brevity prevents an extensive discussion of these action options here. Here's a high level overview.[8]

Risk Management	Uncertainty Mitigation
Market Research	**Scenario planning**
Syndication of Risk Pool	**Playbooks (e.g., Adaptive planning)**
Portfolio Development	**Simulation modeling**
Quantitative "what, if" analysis	**War gaming**
	Future search planning conferences using World Café's

Risk management is a fairly well developed field with numerous reliable methods to aid decision making. We find the mitigation of uncertainty far more interesting. Successful leaders of new ventures need to know how to do scenario planning, what simulation modeling is about, how to design and facilitate future searches (i.e., interactive, multidisciplinary problem solving), and how to facilitate a World Café if they want to effectively deal with uncertainty.

Conclusion

What is there to be learned from our little case studies of dealing with uncertainty? If you step back and generalize the strategy that these three firms used, there is an underlying continuity. Each company acted quickly and aggressively when they realized they faced uncertainty. Don't just sit there, move!

But the scope of their actions varied with the situation. TrashCo used existing product development methods, but put in place a rapid "fail and learn" system. They embarked upon refinement as a strategy. Old Me took it one step further and re-framed the business approach and brand. Lastly, Spookytunes went all out and did a total reinvention. Here is the continuum:

Refine a process--→Reframe a general model -→Reinvent the firm

So, if you are going to ask people to invest in your venture, be prepared to answer questions about how you will manage the risk AND mitigate the uncertainty in your market. Remember,

- Risk management is minimizing the chance of failure when you know the rules of the game.
- Uncertainty is when the rules of the game are changed, AND you don't know what they are.

Knowing the difference between these scenarios and understanding how to take action depending where you are, is, perhaps, the most critical competency an entrepreneur can have today. Do you have it?

We have three major drivers of change but there is a systemic amplifying effect in operation. Just as all these things are going on, something even more basic is happening. We now turn to that structural factor.

New Rules of Economics

__Hear the truth, believe it, practice it (Zen saying)__

It is our contention that the basic underlying social psychology of mutually respected obligations and rules of exchange are undergoing a major change. In other words, the basis of industrial capitalism is crumbling and being replaced with something new.

To begin with, the essence of the protestant ethic is that humans can and should control natural forces to their benefit. That belief is being challenged by an increasing realization that we live on a planet with finite resources. That belief is challenged with increasing frequency of natural disasters. It may be that the rate of said disasters hasn't really changed, just that we are more aware of them.

The flow of the universe is from hard, cold, masculine to soft, warm, feminine. It goes from penetrating to enclosing. And that's where we are, at a cusp of change. Without going off on a metaphysical rant, suffice to say that a shift in belief systems is occurring at an increasing pace[9]. And fear of that change paralyzes action.

Old Rule 1: Constraint on markets creates scarcity. Scarcity raises prices. Cattle as an example. Fewer cows mean higher steak prices.

New Rule: Freedom. Content multiplies at no (or very little) marginal cost. Books are an example. Downloading another copy of a book to a Kindle is almost zero marginal cost. A Kindle costs about $150 no matter if you put 100 or 3000 books on it.

Old Rule 2: Economies of scale reduce marginal costs and therefore price—after a certain investment level in plant/equipment on repetitive processes. For example, once you have paid for the building and equipment the only variable is for raw materials—and perhaps labor these days.

New Rule: No economies of scale because the process of creating "knowledge products," such as articles, books and computer programs are not uniform. Everybody's "app package" is different. There is no cookie cutter answer.

Old Rule 3: Fixed costs reduce uncertainty. Example is of factory production of durable goods. If the cost of my factory is spread out over 40 years, I can accurately forecast my cost of production.

New Rule: Cost of production must be variable, mass customization. The useful half-life of fixed assets becomes less than the time of financing them.

Old Rule 4: Closed markets increase price. Example is monopolistic behavior. Current example is the international market for crude oil and OPEC.

New Rule: Open markets drive down price. Open sourcing of software is an example. Open source products are changed, modified and improved through an informal network of people donating time and intellect for the overall good of the larger user community.

Closing the Space

This is a lot to think about. Changes, changes, changes are everywhere. More uncertainty, new rules no one understands. That's the reality we live with and these are the forces that absolutely require fundamental change at the individual, company and community level. Now we can get to the specifics of how to make changes and see the year 2025 with foresight.

There are two major resources for this chapter. First, an outline of the process we use to help people "discover" what is driving their organization and how to clarify a vision. The second resource at the end of the book is some little hints on how to think your way through this material.

Purpose – What is your purpose?

Reiki symbol Cho Ku Rei meaning "place the power of the universe here". The power is within you, it only needs to be recognized and activated.

Chapter 2 – Purpose: Compass & Gyroscope

"The more you know the less you understand" -- Tao Te Ching

The basic question posed is: "What is your purpose?" This chapter is about being or emotions. It is about how to become more aware, to transform the person of the old reality into the whole person of the new reality. It is about self-gratification and an awakening to our true core. This is a long chapter because we included a step by step description of the phases of transformation here instead of in the resources section. So, let's begin the emotional part of our journey.

Being a part of the change

This chapter is designed to help people make a transition when emotional life becomes more social and less individual.[10] As you move closer and closer to the true digital workplace your capacity to live and work without interacting with others decreases. Many of you have already begun to experience this. Constant email messages, faxes, and phones ringing all the time have placed you in touch with others so much that sometimes it becomes painful.

Your ability to maintain your emotional life as private and personal is rapidly disappearing. Even when you don't want people to intrude into your personal space, they seem to do it. As a result, your emotional life is becoming more social and less individual.

Some of us deal with the increasing pressure to share emotions as an intrusion. People who have these feelings are those that tend to be introverted, and probably like a lot of private time anyway. Others take this increase in amount of connections with others as a pleasant thing. However, even those people, who tend to be extroverted, sometimes find too much interaction and too much questioning about how they feel unpleasant. Even for them, it's possible to reach the email / texting / voicemail / Facebook saturation point!

Another way of saying that our emotional life is becoming more social and less individual with the coming of the digital age is to say that we're becoming more feminine and less masculine. Just as today's management theorists maintain that the collaborative model of organizations that's replacing the old command-and-control approach represents a move away from the male and toward a more female model of work. That is, technology is also enabling, sometimes even imposing, greater female-style interactivity in our emotional lives as well.

The traditional model of how we interact with one another, particularly at work, was based on a premise that your emotional life is something you carry around inside and don't let out into the public eye. This was in part the outgrowth of a mechanical, Western ideology that grew up with the industrial revolution. We see the ideology of privacy in everything from the emphasis on a personal rather than collective relationship with God in some Western religious rituals to our insistence on silence in movie theaters (as if we need to believe we're experiencing something in private even when we're surrounded by hundreds of our fellow human beings).

Most of us find it easy to deal with our emotional life in the context of our family, our immediate friends and our community. They're part of the circle of privacy as that traditional ideology defines it. But somehow, we leave behind this way of relating and dealing with our problems when we enter the workplace. In many organizations the only acceptable forms of emotion are the placid good nature we all show to people we don't know very well and the aggressive anger that still passes for leadership in too many executive suites. It is usually very obvious whenever there is a gathering of emotionally constrained people that they are distracted, unhappy, and not always ready to give their all to the work at hand. Yet with all of those signs of trouble, management's response is clear: "leave your personal problems at the office door." As if by pretending the stresses and strains we brought to the table weren't there, we could go on as a productive, fully functioning organization.

Rather than risk letting their emotions out, people keep silently in meetings, depriving the company of their ideas. To maintain the illusion that they left the emotional turmoil from home at the front door of the company, people trump up work-related problems to vent the anger they were really feeling toward their lives outside of work.

Management's desire to solve emotional problems by pretending they don't exist, is denying the truth that we're all human, and this act of pretending makes it more, not less, difficult for us to get anything done.

The frequency of violence in the workplace, armed violence in the schoolyard, "road rage" and other events that permeate our nightly news has increased in the past few years. Why? These increases of emotional outbursts and the inability to control anger are the final steps on a pathway of industrialization[11]. The pathway has tended to de-humanize everyone in the workplace; therefore, the increased pace of change that technology makes possible lit the fuse to the proverbial powder keg we built when we denied expression of our emotions at work.

The increased pace of change has also augmented our need for stabile and strong relationships. When everything's up in the air, strong emotional bonds give us the strength we need. So, it's ironic that technology, which increases our need for strong social systems to sustain us emotionally, also isolates us physically from each other. For example, telecommuters may be "plugged in" to their fellow workers electronically, but they're usually working alone. Office workers may be surrounded by hundreds of cubicle dwellers like themselves, but most of them spend their time communicating via computer, phone, text and Skype rather than interacting. Much of that communication is message-to-message (email instead of a conversation, voicemail instead of a live chat, a tweet rather than a live Skype session) rather than real-time social exchange.

These old models of workplace behavior make us feel we constantly have to censor ourselves at work; that we're controlled at work by forces outside our power to influence. When we feel this way, we can get anxious and confused. When we are anxious and confused, then we are distracted, not productive; and we probably are not pleasant to live with. Is this the way you planned to live your life? No, we doubt it. However, as many of you know this traditional reality is the <u>reality of today</u>.

Overcoming FUD

We often acquiesce to unhappy situations because, on some level, we prefer them to any alternative we can see. When you accept a situation you don't really like, such as being unhappy at work, there's a good chance that FUD has played a role. FUD, which stands for **f**ear **u**ncertainty and **d**oubt, is a powerful motivator. Where you feel fear, uncertainty, or doubt about change, you stay in the world you know even when you don't much like it.

Table 2-1: FUD

Fear	Uncertainty	Doubt
Basic fears which create absolute panic	What we don't know about the future	In our abilities In our leaders In our deeply held beliefs

If you agree that the traditional, impersonal, workplace isn't something we like, then it's possible that some proportion of fear, uncertainty, and doubt combined to get us to buy that dysfunctional model of work. To better understand this, let us look at what this old way of working gave people that addressed their fears, uncertainties, and doubts.

The most basic fear any of us have is a fear of NOT having an identity; afraid of not knowing who we are or where we fit in to the larger social structure. This basic fear comes out of the struggle we all face in adolescence when we're trying to establish our own being as something separate and unique from our parents, but still within the bounds of the community that we've been born into. The traditional workplace deals with this basic fear by giving us an identity and giving us a community. Consider the classic statement "this is the old company town." We haven't had old company towns for decades now but corporations have continued to provide a sense of identity for their workers.

By providing us with an identity, however limited, the traditional workplace helps us hold the line against a basic human fear. In exchange for the company protecting you from your fear of losing your identify, you agreed to its rules. Primary among these is the rule "leave your emotions at the door." In this environment, the workplace is a purely rational environment, free from the emotional outbursts and irrational urges that drive us when we are not in the workplace. Even though this denial of feelings created problems for you in the workplace; you were willing to pretend it didn't if that meant you could escape the fear of not knowing your place in the world.

The way the traditional company sells us through our uncertainties is also easy to understand. Uncertainty conjures up feelings of anxiety about what the future holds. Recall when you experienced uncertainty. Where will we get the money to pay the rent? How can we afford to send the kids to private school? Or perhaps even more basic for a lot of us, where's the money going to come from to buy food? We dealt with these uncertainties in the traditional way by getting steady employment.

Employment not only provides a concrete way of eliminating basic uncertainties, like how we're going to pay the rent, it also helps us handle uncertainty about what kind of people we want to be in the world. Corporate cultures, those invisible pressures to be and act a certain way, to conform to the overall values of the organization, help us answer questions like "how do I feel about this policy;" "how should I vote in the next election;" "what role should volunteer work play in my life?" "Am I the kind of person who regularly goes to church?"

Whether we're conscious of it or not, corporate cultures include strong messages about the "right" way to act in our communities and at work. These messages go a long way toward helping us reduce psychological and emotional uncertainty as well as physical uncertainty. In exchange for helping us avoid uncertainty, the traditional company expected us to behave in a certain way. The expected behavior included our leaving our feelings at the door, and following its rules.

Doubt is the twin sister of uncertainty. We can feel doubt about our abilities, our leaders and, in some cases, doubt our own deeply held beliefs. The need to avoid feelings of doubt is a powerful motivator. How does the traditional way of working help us deal with doubt?

The corporation helps us overcome doubt in our abilities by providing us with positions of some influence or power. Did you ever wonder why there are so many meetings or why, as Andy Warhol said, everyone gets his fifteen minutes of fame? By providing a forum for people to display their competence, to influence others, or to wield power, meetings are a great way companies make it possible for us to overcome self-doubt. It's hard to doubt your own abilities when people are taking down every word you say!

Similarly, doubt in our leaders is often difficult to admit. One of the reasons we find Dilbert and his pointy-headed manager so funny is that the cartoon directly acknowledges doubt in leadership; a doubt that corporate cultures typically make difficult for us to face. Implicit in the endless stupidities of Dilbert's boss is the truth that in our real jobs we all pretend that our leaders would never act so dumb. And one of the reasons we're all willing to play along with the game at work (denying that the Emperor has no clothes) is that it helps us avoid feelings of doubt in our leaders.

But perhaps the most insidious doubt is that of doubting our deeply held beliefs. What's fair? What's right? This form of doubt addresses our basic issues of integrity, sincerity, and how we treat our fellow human beings. For example, if we believe that people should be rewarded based on the time they spend in companies, and people who are more senior to us deserve respect, then we see behaviors around us that don't support those beliefs, doubt is going to make us very uncomfortable.

The traditional corporate structure makes it easier for us to avoid seeing unfair situations, thus helping us avoid the tension of doubt. As long as companies rewarded loyalty, we could escape having to question if that's the right thing to reward. As long as seniority commanded respect, we could be secure in the knowledge that we'd gain respect the longer we stayed in the same job.

Traditionally, then, companies offered us security: financial and social protection from the vicissitudes of the larger world. In exchange, we agreed to stay put.

When the 1980s ended, the mutual loyalty that made it possible for workers to stay with one company for their entire careers (and for companies to use layoffs as the last resort rather than the first) could no longer protect us from FUD. As a result, we've been newly confronted with thoughts about our place in the world, our values, our beliefs, and our dreams.

Adapt! Through Career Latticing

One of us, Norma by name, has created a systematic program to help people overcome F.U.D. and move into the future. It is a vastly complicated multi-step program that has been field tested and met with considerable success in the workforce development world. So, here are the highlights.

The process is about getting your personal and career development processes in sync with those trends in the larger environment. No going to school to learn how to be a buggy whip maker. The first step is teaching people how to construct their own search engines about economic and workforce trends. Second, people learn how to filter these trends and identify the ones most applicable to them. Third, plan how to close the gaps. Finally, the magic step, where you consciously re-engineer your social network to find and exploit the resources and opportunities you need. That's where our ideas of "guilds," the T.I.E. and the 9E® Leadership processes come in.

As you unravel the DNA strands of our presentation, you anchor your ability to Adapt! through Career Latticing. More detail is presented on the Career Latticing System in the resources section for this chapter. At the individual level this has great implications for chapter 7 when we introduce the idea of a Talent Integration Ecosystem^{sm}. Now back at the ranch.

Getting a grip on Reality "Who are we?"

There are many, many different ways of looking at oneself, running the gamut from astrology to deep psychotherapy. This transition to the New World work requires personal change as well as organizational change. While many of you have been through some sort of personal development training or assessment that was given during a team building exercise, at an organizational development program or perhaps in your own personal quest for better understanding of who you are, what I'm suggesting to you is that any program of self-development needs to begin with some assessment of who you are and how you interact with others. What is YOUR purpose?

The next section of this chapter may be a little confusing for some of you who haven't dealt in the arena of self-development before. I would ask that you suspend judgment by simply going through the material and then reflect back on what it may mean for you or in your particular situation.

Four Critical Questions

There are four critical questions we ask ourselves and our coworkers when we embarked upon a program of change. In the New World of work, where we find ourselves thrown into situations with new coworkers and new bosses almost on a weekly basis, it is important to understand how we interact with others and how they interact with us. Just as the Internet economy has pushed us into a position where it's not "business as usual," the Internet is also pushing us to better understand who we are and how we relate with others so we can more quickly integrate ourselves into these new work teams with a minimum amount of interpersonal friction.

The chart that follows outlines the four basic questions with brief descriptions of how these things are going to change in our New

World. The discussion that follows the chart briefly outlines why this is important and how it's going to affect you personally in the New World of work.

Table 2-2: The Four Critical Elements

What's important	How it's going to change
How do you process information?	There will be more of it and it will come more quickly
How do you interact with others?	These interactions will be separated in time and space
How do you deal with conflict?	There will be more diversity in your social worlds
What motivates you? (or Where do you get your motivation?)	You will need to know where to go to get it

How do you Process Information?

We all process information differently. Information processing is one of the key tasks that all of us, especially knowledge workers, perform in the workplace. As our work changes from manual labor to intellectual labor processing information becomes our eyes, ears, and our fingers on our hands of the workplace.

Understanding how we, and those around us, process information is critical simply because this activity in our merging workplace is increasing. The ability to read faster, manipulate numbers, and use graphics to express ideas is coming at us at a blistering pace. I'm sure you know someone who has the ability to concentrate while shutting out everything else around them.

Issues arise when different members of a work team have different styles of processing information and they don't appreciate the value that each of these different styles brings to the team. So, when a person who can concentrate intensely works with a person who likes to scan the horizon they probably will irritate each other at times. Just as understanding how individuals process information differently, it is important to understand how different workgroups perform the same task.

For example, if you ever sat in on a meeting that involved people from engineering and people from marketing you know what I'm talking about. The people from marketing tend to see a broad picture, longtime horizons and they speak in images. People from engineering see numbers, they prefer details and they tend to be explicit. Helping individuals in these two groups understand how they process information differently, goes a long way towards improving their effectiveness. We have successfully helped them appreciate their differences by having them describe how they process information with each other.

Sometimes this process is uncomfortable because they are beginning to open up to others, discuss their differences and try to appreciate those differences. The workplace of old implicitly prohibited this kind of open, intimate discussion. The workplace of the future will not only permit such activity but also encourage it. As AI (Artificial Intelligence) personality and communication profiling gains wider acceptance, if you do not know yourself intimately, then the company likely will. Armed with this deep insight the company will make your hiring, team assignment and career advancement decisions for you.

How We Interact with Others?

Interacting with others in the New World of work is going to be more difficult than it has been. These interactions will be spread out in time and space; we cannot depend on sensing the "nonverbal" and other signals as when we are meeting face-to-face. Our interactions will be more ambiguous and difficult to interpret.

In the traditional world of work, we were hired and assigned to a department or work team without much regard to our personality or our style of interaction. We'd been taught from early childhood that we needed to learn how to get along with people and "don't take it personally." Those days are rapidly disappearing. As the Internet opens New Worlds to us and we find we can pick and choose the projects and the people we want work with, we need to understand how we interact with each other.

Actually, we will start living in two worlds. The "real" physical world of our communities in parallel with a virtual one. A new skill is to recognize which one you are in and how to appropriately interact in that world. We need to become "bi-lingual" in a new sense. Social network sites, for example, will actually allow us to be more intimately and closely connected than ever before.

How we interact with others is closely tied to how we process information. But it's more than that. Some people are more aggressive and others are more passive. Some folks are more outgoing and others are more reserved. There's a whole host of these different dimensions and each of us falls someplace on the dimensions. Interpreting different styles of interacting as meaning something more than they really do, creates frustration in work teams. For example, people who were more contemplative may want to listen to information and take some time before they react to it. This may seem like a simple thing but how does this taking time to mull something over, appear to a person who is used to quick and rapid interaction? I think they would become frustrated.

The quick person may interpret the contemplative person's behavior as signaling lack of respect, lack of importance or lack of concern. They're thinking "why didn't they respond" and start misinterpreting behavior. Alternatively, the contemplative person is probably thinking "why is he always in such hurry?" He may feel frustrated by the pressure to react quicker than he wants to.

In a face-to-face environment, this can be bad enough but when you extend it to interaction over the Internet, it can become critical. So, I send an email to a colleague in Europe and I'm the kind of person who expects and appreciates rapid interaction. The person in Europe, being more contemplative in nature, receives my message and decides to go to a long lunch and think about the message before responding. Or perhaps, in their normal course of interaction, he takes a day or two to ponder my email before formulating an answer to the question or the problem.

How Do I Deal with Conflict?

Conflict is a fact of life. We all deal with it every day at different levels and with different people. In the workplace of the future dealing with conflict becomes more of an issue because diversity in the workplace increases. Different value systems, realities, beliefs, and worldviews all get brought into the new workplace and they present new situations to deal with.

The word conflict seems to have a negative connotation in our everyday use; but not all conflict is bad. If we reframe it and look at these differences in perspectives, ways of processing information and ways of interacting with one another, it takes on a different and more positive light. So understanding how we tend to deal with conflict becomes important.

One way of dealing with conflict is to simply avoid it. Avoiding conflicts in cyberspace is much easier than it is in face-to-face situations because you get to choose whom you talk to and when you talk to them. How many of you screen your calls? Or, maybe you simply delete messages from your voice mail when you hear who they are from? All of the ways we control the flow of information coming at us can also be used to avoid dealing with situations we find unpleasant and conflict laden.

This is perhaps the most uncomfortable aspect of interpersonal behavior that we all have to deal with. The first step in dealing with conflict is to realize that it exists. Use a third party facilitator to help deal with serious conflict in workgroups. Once we are engaged in conflict, it is very difficult to realize the part each of us has played in creating the situation and significantly change our own behavior to resolve the issue.

The strength the facilitator brings to this situation is their ability to disengage emotionally from the situation and objectively assess differences in styles, opinions and approaches that may be contributing to the situation at hand. In the Internet world, this is difficult to do because you're already separated in time and space.

However, we are beginning to see the emergence of a new social role in these work situations, which deserves close attention.

The best example that we all know about is the use of a moderator, or host of chat rooms and bulletin boards. The major function they serve is to monitor conflict situations and help resolve them quickly before it destroys the entire quality of the conversation. This moderator, or facilitator role, is one, which I believe is becoming increasingly important in our new world of work. It's a skill set and talent that needs to be developed and probably will come to us from a more traditional background of an organizational development specialist or psychologist.

Where do I Get my Motivation?

Motivation is a tough issue. Different things motivate us; some are motivated by money, some by fame, and others by glory. Politicians relish in power and business people think about making profits. And, some are motivated by deeply held beliefs. Nonetheless, we are all motivated by something while a lack of motivation leads to dissatisfaction with our work life and eventually leads to burnout.

People's motivation in compensation systems need to be tied closely together or they won't work. Putting a person who's motivated by security in a high-risk situation is asking for disaster. The new work teams that we are forming are complex pictures of different motivations. Being able to understand and identify motivators is critical to the success of these new work teams. It often falls to the leader to determine what these motivations are and make sure they are all satisfied as best they can be.

Our motivations inform our very basic approach to life. They get to what our passion really is. What you love to do? Answering that kind of question can get to the heart of what our motivations really are. What you live for? That's another excellent question to ask. Motivations draw us into situations because we sense that by doing that, being there, or working with that group we will be satisfied at some deeper level.

In the workplace of the future, there is a significant distinction between "a job" and the work we like to do. The job is a set of tasks that we've performed in order to receive a paycheck. Work is something we do because we find it intrinsically satisfying; it then serves as a self-motivator. Not that we would work for no pay, but we certainly find other characteristics of work that are more satisfying. In the first chapters of this book we discussed the changing face of the new worker and the factors that motivate people even more than traditional pay.

We can go even deeper than that to understand what the bases factors are that motivate us. At some level, this gets to understanding what our true purpose is and why we were put in this world. This book is not the place for that level of philosophic discussion but it may be a topic that you can pursue at some time for yourself. We provided references in the last chapter this book to assist you on your journey.

Build Your Own Bridges, Be Your Own Pilot

Now let us return to the fundamental question of this chapter: what is my purpose? We presented several different ways of looking at yourself in order to answer the four basic questions of transition: how you process information, interact with others, deal with conflict and where your motivation comes from. Although this is well and good as a general guideline, it still doesn't give you specific actions you can take to embark on your transition process. Making the transition to the new world of work is not easy; specific actions will facilitate your process.

The future of work, at its core, is about a process of continuous change. Change at the individual level, at the organizational level, and at the community level. You need an adaptable plan. You need a map. You need some guidelines about how to go through this transition process not once, not twice but quite probably a minimum of six to ten times during your professional work life.

There are two basic, concrete things you need to do to ensure your transformation process is on-going and effective. You need to build the basic functioning capability to continuously change and stay in-sync with your business environment, your self and your community. The two things you can do are:

Become your own gyroscope

Becoming your own gyroscope means you start taking your "sense of correction" internally instead of externally. The shift here is how we talk about where purpose comes from; is your purpose, orientation, and your gyroscope inside of you? Or, is it a "purpose" given to you by an external organization or group? You need to learn how to follow your own advice. That is not to say that we won't seek out new knowledge, opinions and guidance from others; but you will do it in a way that only *forms part of your motivation - - it doesn't become your motivation*.

Personal Board of Directors

In a company, the Board of Directors functions as a governance council. It's a place where long-term strategic and change oriented decisions get made. It stays above the everyday foray of operations. It's a place where executives can go and seek council concerning serious and long-lasting actions they are contemplating. It is ultimately the place where the long-term health of the organization is maintained.

This "board" is your governance structure. We have used Personal Boards for over twenty years and they have never failed us – especially at critical times. Through both good times and bad, with 20/20 hindsight our boards were critical in helping us make the transitions successfully. Now use the idea for 20/25 Foresight. Detailed instructions on board composition, selection, how to remove them and how to upgrade your membership are in the "Tools and Resources" chapter at the end of this book.

12 New Skills – What do you need to be able to do?

Leadership. Symbolizes three levels of existence and the need for leaders to bring these levels together. Many places of origin among Norse tribes and West African religions.

Chapter 3 – New Skills: Leadership for the 21st Century

> "You cannot solve a problem from the same consciousness that created it. You must learn to see the world anew."
> - Albert Einstein

The basic question posed in this chapter is: "What are the specific new competencies required to be an effective leader in the 21st century?" This chapter is about the ego. What do "I" have to do before I am ready to lead? It is about self-definition and learning how to use power as a force for good.

Backstory

There are many forces pushing organization to radically change the way they operate. This new business model requires a new kind and style of leadership. This chapter outlines those forces for change and a new paradigm of leadership development. This chapter is a contribution to the overall thrust of this book—that radically new and different skills and competencies are needed to build a sustainable you and community in the 21st century.

- The leadership skills that worked in the industrial era don't work today. This is a conceptual world, not a machine world. New leadership skills will be needed in a global, interconnected world. Facilities managers can be at the forefront of this revolution, if they prepare themselves.

- Effective leadership for the 21st century begins with an internal, personal transformation. You can't change an organization until the leaders change. It starts with each person and their transformation.

- The skills and competencies needed are knowable, and can be taught through experience. This isn't rocket science. Tried and true principles of social psychology can help prepare our future leaders. And, this psychology is valid across cultures in today's global business environment.

Forces shaping change

We've been writing for the last two years about the on-rushing wave of fundamental change that is sweeping over the old industrial order of our world. We believe that what is occurring, that also has everyone's thoughts and fears all twisted up is more than a routine swing in the "business cycle." No less an expert than Jeff Immelt, CEO of General Electric said it best: "Someone hit the re-set button." We've expanded on that by suggesting that a "re-structuring" of many industries is impending.

For example we have Jim Clifton, Gallup's chairman and CEO, saying that businesses have squeezed as much as they can out of the old industrial model of business organization. Management fads such as such as Six Sigma, reengineering, and total quality management have peeked out in their ability to improve organizational performance. So, what's next? We believe the next frontier, the moon shot if you will, is quite simply leadership. But the questions remain - What is it, how is it practiced, and how do people learn to be leaders of the 21st century?

Let's look at a couple of expert opinions. First from the Herman Group, a highly respected authority in human resource management:

> "What worked for organizations pre–recession just isn't sustainable in today's environment. The current business environment affects the supply and demand of talent in unprecedented ways, as well as the ability of employers to engage and retain employees. Employers must respond to the revised "employee-employer contract" and employees' evolving priorities. They must alter how they operate and how people may connect to their companies and work. "[12]

These factors are not limited to the private sector. In fact, we believe the leadership "crisis" will first appear in the public sector when revenues decline by 25-33% in the next year. Specifically, communities that have been relatively homogenous since WWII are being forced to change the way they think and behave by three major forces. We discussed these forces in the first chapter. This discussion is about what you, as a leader, need to do to survive and thrive today.

Tomorrow, the crisis will shift to tradecraft and next generation knowledge workers.

Brief history of Leadership Development

Let us start with a quick look at how this issue of developing new leaders for modern times was addressed. Wikipedia say it best:

> "Traditionally, leadership development has focused on developing the leadership abilities and attitudes of individuals. Different personal characteristics can help or hinder a person's leadership effectiveness and require formalized programs for developing leadership competencies http://en.wikipedia.org/wiki/Leadership_development - cite_note-1 yet; everyone can develop their leadership effectiveness. Achieving such development takes focus, practice and persistence more akin to learning a musical instrument than reading a book."[13]

Traditionally, Leadership Development (LD) has been focused on the individual level. It has been assumed that success in development is tied to three variables:

- Individual learner characteristics—such as temperament or personality

- Quality of the leadership development program—the military does it best

- Support from upper management levels—both in terms of money and social support

Further, most formal programs contain similar elements.

- They integrate many developmental experiences over an extended time period (e.g. 12-18 months)

- They are based on experiential learning

- They are founded on a principle of self-efficacy. That is people are taught to believe that their efforts can have an effect on the organization

- They originate from an ability to develop a clear vision of the desired state and this vision is communicated effectively

We are not suggesting that this approach is without merit. It certainly has worked well for decades. Entire organizations and numerous consulting practices have been built upon this model; for example, the renowned the Center for Creative Leadership and others[14]. However, many authorities in the field have come recently, to question the efficacy of continuing to use this model for leadership development.[15] Likewise, we believe that the time has come for a new model of leadership development—one based on the realities of the forces shaping our society as we enter the 21st century.

New ways of thinking required

We've intimated that the world, which is emerging, is more interconnected, global and collaborative than what predominated over our (Western) culture over the past two centuries. The fundamental cognitive shift that is occurring is from a straight, linear, predictable world to a curvilinear, systemic, uncertain world. We have to begin looking at how we think, and perceive the world around us. Jake Chapman describes it well:

> "Most people are not aware of how they think. This is not because they are unintelligent, it is because their mode of thinking has evolved over many years, has served them well and does not need to be examined or questioned. Most people are unaware of the degree to which they use mechanical images and metaphors. They are also unaware of the degree to which their fear of loss of control and uncertainty maintains their commitment to, and belief in, control and predictability. Individuals only become aware of these facets of how they operate either in crises or as a result of deliberate self-inspection."[16]

If this were the case, how would one go about developing a new leadership development program that takes all of this into account?

We believe that a leadership development program for experienced managers can be designed to develop the skills, knowledge and understanding that will enable them to move their organizations towards relevance and sustainability for the next decade.

The basic assumption we hold is that organizations cannot become relevant and sustainable until their leaders develop the mental flexibility and competencies necessary to deal with the uncertainties of the future. This new program is not a traditional change management program.

This is about transformation—not transactions.

Fundamental transformation has four basic dimensions: it is irreversible, it challenges traditional assumptions, it changes your identity, and it shifts the purpose of the organization. The model we have in mind leads a person through several stages of transformational change: (Note: this is the same evolutionary model we used in the previous chapter on changing purpose)

- Launch: What is it that I am so anxious about?
- Connection: Is it me or is everyone else around here crazy?
- Dividing: What do I need to serve that is larger than me?
- Agreement: What mental state do I need to be in?
- Approaching: What help do I need and where do I go get it?
- Dismissal: How to get rid of the old baggage?
- Achievement: Waking up

What are the new skills and abilities embedded in this program? We group learning's into three basic categories: functional, expressive and motivational skills. Specially, they are defined as:

Table 3-1 New Skills

Functional	Expressive	Motivational
➤ Future thinking ➤ Drivers of change ➤ New Patterns of action ➤ Design Processes	➤ Asking Questions ➤ Systems Thinking ➤ Balance, Flow and Circularity ➤ Personal Identity	➤ Living Out Leadership ➤ Spirituality and Change ➤ Presence of Self ➤ Transformation

In summary, a Leadership Development program for the 21st century consists of seven stages of transformation change, which contain 12 discrete new competencies, or skill sets. Briefly, they are:

Future thinking: The ability to anticipate events in the larger context of your business. Future thinkers have the ability to do "what if" scenarios in a three to five year timeframe. For example, what would be the impact on your business if energy prices quadrupled?

Drivers of change: The ability to recognize the multi-disciplinary nature of change. Drivers of change have a broad perspective of the elements that shape human behavior in both rational and irrational ways including technology, economics, politics and cultural aspects.

New patterns of action: Leaders have the ability to move beyond simple "cause and effect" relationships. They have the ability to visualize alternative organizational structures and forms and also an understanding of the utility of using different forms in different situations.

Design processes: An understanding of design as a process that can be consciously applied in changing situations. Knowledge of how to move from a wide array of configurations to a smaller set of options using functionality, cost and aesthetic filters.

Asking questions: An ability to engage in critical thinking is the ability to know what the critical questions are to ask as you move up a hierarchy of "unreflective thinker" to "master thinker." Inquisitive leaders know and understand how to apply universal intellectual standards.

Systems thinking: Seeing the pattern that connects. Systems relationships include feedback, feed forward, attenuation, and amplification. They understand the links between environment, internal operations and information flows.

Balance, flow and circularity: An understanding of the pattern to the flow of energy (including information); the ability to balance positive and negative forces and their reconciliation. The capacity to understand a larger context the leader and the organization is connected.

Living out leadership: Everyday living out the principles of leadership: integrity of action. They demonstrate empathy, loyalty, and discretion in action; living out high moral and ethical standards.

Spirituality and change: An understanding, appreciation and acceptance of the spiritual aspects of life. Service is in the interest of others and the community they are members of. They have appreciation of the principle of "stewardship" resources and the environment.

Presence of self: Understanding how others view you in action while also living in the moment. A sense of the dramatic and ability of actions and words to influence others attitudes and shape their behavior.

Transformation: An understanding, and a sincere desire, for what is required to fundamentally change. Never going back, never looking the same, having a different fundamental identity and being in service. They tune into their calling.

Cultural Differences in Leadership

Leadership Development in the 21st century is also global. This implies skills need to be cross cultural—and not rooted in a narrow geo-political perspective. The program we are proposing in this chapter is designed to be "meta-cultural" in perspective and equally applicable in North America, Europe, South America and Asia.

One of the foremost experts on cross-cultural communications is Geert Hofstede. His studies point out several psychological universals that relate to the practice of leadership:

1. Relation of the individual to authority
2. Concept of self, especially:
    a. Relationship between individual and society
    b. Individual's concept of masculinity and femininity
3. Ways of dealing with conflict including aggression and emotionality[17]

Our development program incorporates these universal issues. In fact, several of the units of instruction are designed primarily from an Eastern philosophical context to give leaders sensitivity to these central issues as a function of the culture they operate within.

Examples of coming challenges

We recognize that this is fine theory, but so what? Let me give you an example of trends in the real estate world that will bring this into focus. First, you will be managing a portfolio that is considerably smaller than today's holdings. We, among others, believe that the process by which commercial real estate is designed and built is broken. Decreases in productivity and waste in the process cost owners 50% more than necessary. Financing new construction is doomed without significant changes in the PROCESS. We anticipate management pressure to reduce real estate portfolios by as much as 50% within five years. Forward leaning companies such as IBM and H-P are already moving in that direction. How will you respond?

Rex Miller and his team[18] produced a masterpiece detailing the broken process by which we currently design and construct our commercial buildings. Simply put it doesn't work and the banks that write checks, or underwrite corporations, are beginning to realize that half of their money goes down a black hole—never to be recovered. So, what is the scope of the problem? It is huge. In 2007, the commercial AEC (architects, engineering and construction) industry was netting 1.28 Trillion dollars in the US. Half of that money was wasted because of the process in place. If we come down from 50K feet, the average project is $6 Million. But that means that $3 Million on average goes out the back door.

The problem, in essence, is an old industrial business process that is linear in form, composed of many disconnected pieces that are sub-optimized on a cost basis. The world has become more complex, interrelated, and faster in pace over the past 50 years. These three forces broke the standard model that worked well in slower paced times.

The typical business model for commercial construction optimizes on cost, schedule and quality. You can have two of the three, but never all three. You want high quality (say a design that meets a business need) then you come in over budget and are late. Suffice to say many factors contribute to this breakdown. Rex highlights a few for us:

1. Risk adverse architects (probably a dying breed by the way)

2. Legal processes which are murky at best

3. A cost estimating process built on inaccuracies

4. Lack of up front business cases

The solution is simple actually but extremely difficult to implement. This is why new leadership is required. Miller likes to use an analogy of a compass and a gyroscope. In the world of yesterday a compass was an effective way to guide you on a journey. Every once in a while you would stop, take another reading, adjust your course and move on. Repeat the process at frequent intervals. But today's world requires a gyroscope that is dynamic and continuously self-corrects to allow for constantly changing conditions.

Playbook for Implementation

The major barrier to developing a sustainable organization or community at this point is a polity that lacks basic competencies to pull organizations forward in the direction of societal evolution. That direction, by the way, is towards continuously greater connectivity, harmony of relations among different groups, and the recognition of unity of purpose. But most leaders today don't know what they don't know. Thanks to Socrates for giving us a way to think instead of being told what to do.

Our outline for a Leadership Development program can best be described as a set of questions that training would help you answer. So, I like to phrase those capacities in the form of being able to answer some key questions:

1) How should you think about the future?

2) What forces are driving these fundamental changes?

3) What would new patterns of behavior and action look like?

4) What can we learn from the process of design to help us continuously adapt?

5) Are we asking the right critical questions?

6) Are you able to think systemically at a higher level of complexity?

7) How do we achieve balance in flows of energy and information?

8) What is the core of my personal identity as a leader?

9) How can I live this vision out?

10) How do others perceive me in a leadership role?

The formal program consists of a series of eight workshops structured around the seven stages of transformation outlined above, plus an introduction to the process. As we mentioned earlier, this approach also focuses on teams of leaders, not individuals, so it is critical that whole leadership teams participate together so they learn to function as a highly effective group.

An Eastern Perspective on Leadership

Before we wrap up with some ideas of how you will know when you arrived, I want to return to central theme of this book: globalization of leadership. As we mentioned earlier, there are some cultural universals to leadership competencies. But, let me be more specific here.

One of the most well-known Eastern philosophies on leadership has been "The Art of War" by Sun Tzu. We humbly suggest that just as we can apply Eastern thought into the Western world, we can do the reverse.[19] For example, when you closely examine the content of Leadership Development 2.0 learning units they correlate with the ancient Chinese concepts of Yin and Yang.

Table 3-2: Yin/Yang Leadership

Yin	Yang
Female, passive, dark	Male, aggressive, light
• Design Process	• Future thinking
• Drivers of change	• New patterns of action
• Balance, flow and circularity	• Asking questions
• Personal Identity	• Systems thinking
• Presence of Self	• Living out leadership
• Transformation	• Spirituality and change

Brevity prohibits in depth discussion of the cross-cultural applicability of the leadership development program proposed here. Suffice to say, the structure and content was developed with equal recognition of the validity of a broad array of cultural philosophies.

How do you make it work?

- Commit to a process of transformation and seek out external resources to guide you through the process. We recommend you spend one day each week learning and practicing new ways of working. Start with building a new support network.

- Engage in a self-assessment process. Focus on finding out what you do best. What are your strengths? You can't plan your journey unless you know where you are starting. The first step is an honest evaluation of your strengths and weaknesses.

- Begin building a business case. If you were 20% more productive, if your team was 40% more productive; what would be the financial impact on your business? You can't sell your boss an investment of money and your time unless you can show what results will occur.

How will you know when you get there?

How do you know you have made the transformation? There is no examination, no test you can take. People report that when they are presented with a new problem or situation, they find themselves behaving in non-habitual ways.

New ways of thinking, new ways of seeing the world are more sensed, than seen. It is helpful to have a small group of advisors who have some history with you. They will be the ones to tell you, you are doing things differently.

One very specific technique, which is effective, is personal journaling. Keep a journal on a weekly basis (daily is better if you have the time). Note self-reflections of your actions, thoughts and attitudes. Reflecting back on this journal will help you spot trends and changes. Underlying one of the critical new leadership skills, transformation, is an ability to do self-reflection and self-observation. Develop the ability to self-monitor; you no longer need external validation of your leadership behavior. You will know when you are there. Look inside Grasshopper.

The other technique we recommend is to examine in detailed every few months where you are putting your energy. We tend to equate "busyness" with progress and accomplishment. If we are putting our energy into things that don't help us realize our true purpose, then it is largely wasted. We have a matrix tool in the resources section for this chapter that will assist you in making those periodic checkups.

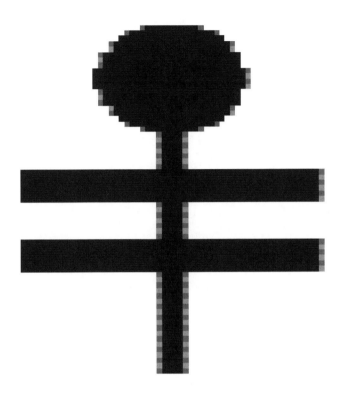

Artisans of Thought – Who you will be

The dragonfly is from Hopi traditions. There is a double meaning here. It represents an ability to get past self-imposed limits and achieve new goals. On the other hand, the dragonfly represents quickness, agility and invincibility.

Chapter 4 – Artisans of Thought

"Grass doesn't try to grow, it just grows. Fish don't try to swim, they just swim. Flowers don't try to bloom, they just bloom."

- Deepak Chopra, the Seven Spiritual Laws of Success

The basic question posed is: "What does the Future of Work look like from the perspective of the worker-person?" This is the "heart" of our story. It is about the person who has come to self-acceptance and love for their fellow workers. Its color is green. It is about how you can become your own person and energize the social network cloud that surrounds us all. In fact, with minimal effort you can design, create and nourish your own network.

This chapter has five parts that will lead you to the realization of your true potential. This story is about Artisans of Thought (also referred to as AOT and simply Artisan). Artisans are the next generation; they will create economic and social value in our global society. The story unfolds in five integrated parts: 1) who they are; 2) what they do; 3) how are they unique; 4) how they organize themselves; and 5) how they act upon the world.

The story is intended for the Artisans themselves, and also for those who are interested in meeting the needs of our new society. Choose the parts that are most important to you, but read the whole story so you know how all the parts working together will create economic and social value for our global society.

Who they are?

Some argue that the "job titles" of the future don't exist today. That's because the "jobs" that will have value have not been invented yet.[20] We would argue that the very idea of a "job" is outmoded and fading away. However, that is a topic for another day. For now, consider one emerging group of people whose actions create the highest amount of relative value to society: Artisans of Thought.

Artisans are those in our society who continuously apply creativity and invention. They take what is inside their minds and hearts and give it expression. Usually they are seen as different, unique and sometimes living on the boundaries of conventional social mores.

I can only imagine that in ancient times these were the shamans and tribal medicine men. In todays, post-industrial world, they often gravitate towards the arts, sciences and the most innovative discipline: design.

The problem we have with 'them - these Artisans- is we don't know what to call them. Artisans are the transformers among us; as such they don't have job titles or recognized positions of status and power in today's world.[21] We don't, yet, have a language and grammar to talk about them. Think about it. Societal and cultural advances often travel far ahead of contemporary culture. What would you have called an airline pilot in 1650 AD?

Artisans will be the future primary "value adders" in today's economic jargon.[22] O.K., why? Because they have the talents and the unique transformational abilities to achieve things that computers and technology can't currently, accomplish.

Robots can farm, build cars and vacuum a living room. Computers can crunch numbers, routinize and automate stable, known processes and play chess rather well. But can they go beyond the known? Can they invent? Can they design? And, most importantly, can Robots alone create innovative designs and apply them in a way that adds transformative value to society? I don't think so, and that's why Artisans present the evolutionary cutting edge of human development.

Let me link this thinking to other current students of the human condition. Richard Florida coined the term "the creative class" back in 2002.[23]

> "Super-Creative Core: This group comprises about 12 percent of all U.S. jobs. It includes a wide range of occupations (e.g. science, engineering, education, computer programming, research), with arts, design, and media workers forming a small

subset. Florida considers those belonging to this group to 'fully engage in the creative process.' The Super-Creative Core is considered innovative, creating commercial products and consumer goods. The primary job function of its members is to be creative and innovative. 'Along with problem solving, their work may entail problem finding.'

<u>Creative Professionals</u>: These professionals are the classic knowledge-based workers and include those working in healthcare, business and finance, the legal sector, and education. They 'draw on complex bodies of knowledge to solve specific problems' using higher degrees of education to do so."

It seemed earth-shaking work at the time. It was wonderful because it got people thinking about what kind of economic activity really added value in a (then) emerging information- based global economy.

Another example of an Artisan is best-selling author Daniel Pink. Daniel has written several books, which flit around the edges of the idea being presented here. And frankly, his work has always been an inspiration. Free Agent Nation in 2001; A Whole New Mind in 2005 and now Drive in 2010.

In A Whole New Mind, Dan introduced a set of six new "senses" he maintained were the basis for the required masteries of the "conceptual age". They were design, story, symphony, empathy, play and meaning. Not wanting to steal Dan's thunder, but suffice to say, these abilities really describe the core competencies of what we call the Artisan with literary license, my interpretation:

> **Design** is not just function; it is the aesthetic quality of a thing - be it a chair, a house, or a town. For a community, design is a combination of architecture, appealing public and natural spaces, layout, and geography.
>
> **Story** is not just argument; it is the compelling narrative. It's the engaging and emotional part of the conversation.
>
> **Symphony** is not just focus; but variation, interweaving of

things, putting it all together across boundaries and synthesizing things.

Empathy is not just logic; it is about caring for others, understanding their various motivations, and identifying with them as part of a larger whole.

Play is not just seriousness; it is humor, lightheartedness, and games.

Meaning is not just consumerism and possession of material things; it is about purpose, transformation, and spiritual fulfillment.

[4] Daniel Pink, *A Whole New Mind: Moving from the Information Age to the Conceptual Age*, The Berkeley Publishing Group, 2005.

When you take Florida's "super creative core" and Dan's six new "senses" you start to get a rough description of this emergent class of economic actors of the future. But, instead of spending more time trying to figure out what to call them, let's look at what they do.

What they do?

In a world where advanced degrees in professional disciplines are rapidly becoming a commodity, prosperity belongs to individuals with the ability to react with agility to unpredictable market forces, data, and events.[24]

Well, that's the textbook definition of Artisans in action. They help others react (or hopefully, be proactive) and be more agile. Remember the central purpose, the moral compass if you will, of these Artisans is to apply their abilities and talents to helping others enjoy a better life, experience the world in a more positive way or bring meaning to where none existed before.

Artisans of Thought transform ideas into a reality, which can be sensed, experienced and used by others, who are without the Artisan's viewpoint and skills. Before I list, a few examples, consider what transformation really is:

Fundamental transformation has four basic dimensions: it is irreversible, it challenges traditional assumptions, it changes your identity, and it shifts the purpose of the person or organization being transformed. Let's dissect each of those from the vantage point of the Artisan.

- Irreversible: like a butterfly from a caterpillar. The butterfly can never go back to being a caterpillar. Metamorphosis doesn't go backwards.

- Challenges assumptions: once transformed the world doesn't work the way it used to.

- Changes identity: It looks different, and is seen as such by others.

- Shifting purpose: It is motivated and strives towards a different goal.

Artisans are about this central task of transformation. Consider these examples:

1. A healer is a person that works to transform a person from a state of illness to a state of wellness. When practiced in an ethical manner the patient can't go back to being ill (unless they choose to do so by not heading the prescribed regimen). Assumptions of behavior are changed. Different diets, patterns of lifestyle and practices. The patient looks different—more healthy and alive. Finally, purpose changes to continuously strive for a state of health. Anyone who has ever witnessed a person overcome an addiction or survive a life threatening illness has seen this in practice.

2. A scientist or more specifically a mathematician. This Artisan may have a special understanding of geometry and calculus. They transform those equations into calculations, which follow underlying descriptions of basic physics, into formulas and tables.

These can be used to guide airplanes or rocket ships to their destinations. It's unlikely that the user of those tools could go back and develop the original theory. The world works in a simpler, predictable fashion; it's not mysterious, it's "understood"; and purpose has gone from the beauty of mathematics to helping people find their way on a journey.

3. Lastly, the Artisan themself. This Artisan is the master of expression. They see patterns, relationships and experience emotions in a profound way. Their talent is transforming their inner experience into something to be experienced by others. They are transforming the invisible into the visible. Now think of the last time you experienced a work of art (a sculpture, a movie, a song, a story). Once done you were in a state that you couldn't reverse; you see the world through a different lens of perception; you are a different person, and if it was a very powerful piece, you walk a different path towards appreciation of an aesthetic.

How are they unique?

I suggest that the future economy will be dominated by this emerging category of "worker". The older generations are our proxy for the vanishing industrial work model, and the younger ones prototypes of a society dominated by Artisans of Thought. Let me offer a word of caution here. Not all younger generation people are going to be Artisans. However, I would suggest they have a higher probability of becoming an Artisan. So, to get a focus on what's different about this cohort, a look at the "coming" generation proves illustrative.

Artisans are relatively well educated, have significant practical experience, are well connected and are focused on their purpose. These are the characteristics, which separate them from the workforce in general. Moreover, they are conscious of these characteristics and actively work to improve these qualities. Let's look at each of them in turn.

This group is best characterized in today's society by the so-called millennial generation, those 18-29 years old. They are more educated (on average) than older generations at a comparable time in their lives. Look at the comparison from a recent Pew Survey. Percentages are a total of "some college" and "4 Year degrees"[25]

Table 4-1: Pew Research Survey

	Males	Females
Millennial	49	60
Gen X'ers	46	52
Boomers	38	34

We can only conclude that we are going to have more Artisans in future generations than we have had. Interestingly, women have taken the lead by a very impressive number. One can only speculate what social relationship changes will accompany women taking a dominant role in the economic sector.

Another uniqueness of Artisans is that they not only have formal education, but practical experience. Just as it wasn't enough for a stonemason in the 15th century to have the requisite technical skills, but they had to publicly demonstrate their craft. Artisans seek out opportunities to "show what they can do". And like any good Artisan, they assemble a portfolio of work. You need not look much further than the social media to see evidence of this in the form of video resumes and personal websites.

Although the number of internship opportunities has increased over the years, there seems to be some exploitation going on among our budding millennial Artisans.[26] It appears that the general recessionary inversion in the labor supply and demand equation has led to this situation. The point is that a formal education is longer enough to demonstrate your worth in the labor market. You have to be able to show it through experience.

Seems like a chicken and egg problem. But it's not really. If your value system places a primacy on "doing your thing", then seeking out experience opportunities is second nature. Volunteer or public service, experience education, or a stint in the military all lends Artisans to developing this competency.

They are connected. 61% of millenials use social networking sites on a daily basis as compared to only 32% for Baby Boomers.[27] This level of connectivity has not gone unnoticed by the business community. Look at this quote from a prominent business strategy journal.[28]

> *"We call them Generation C — connected, communicating, content-centric, computerized, and community-oriented, always clicking. As a rule, they were born after 1990 and lived their adolescent years after 2000. By 2020, they will make up 40 percent of the population in the U.S., Europe, and the BRIC countries, and 10 percent of the rest of the world — and by then, they will constitute the largest single cohort of consumers worldwide."*

In just 8 years, they will be the dominant cultural force on this planet.

The last distinguishing characteristic of Artisans is their personal focus. Being creative, giving something back to the community or pursuing a career off the "beaten path as Thoreau would say is not always financially rewarding—at least at first. We have all heard of the starving artist, the wandering poet.

As more and more people move into the artisan role consumerism will vanish. Already we can see this shift occurring across the generations. Boomers are motivated by compensation and a desire for responsibility. Quite the contrary our Millenials prefer "free time" to pursue whatever strikes their fancy and an opportunity to advance them based on merit.[29] It's about their purpose. If you are an employer, you had better determine their purpose and show them how that can be related to your firm's purpose. And if it's just money, you don't stand a chance.

How do they organize themselves?

Historically workers organized themselves around issues of common interest. They lived out the strategy that there was strength in numbers. The prototypical workers organization in the industrial era was the labor union. But that won't work for Artisans. The war for talent is over and talent won.

I believe the primary organizing form for Artisans will be something akin to medieval guilds. Guilds and 'confederations' will return as the primary social organizational model for these smaller groups of people. Guilds will be responsible for recruitment of talent, some training (more like mentoring) and enforcement of process quality standards. Guilds will be based on a common interest in a particular topic area, or expertise such as the Screen Actors Guild.[30] This brief introduction of guilds is intended to ground you in the idea. We will return with a more lengthy discussion and analysis in Chapter 6.

Professor Tom Malone, from MIT, probably states this best:

> *"You could call these things societies or networks or clubs or associations. But the word that we liked best was guilds — harking back to the medieval craft guilds. The basic idea is that, as an independent worker, you could join a guild which would give you a kind of home - a stable home as you moved from job to job, company to company, employer to employer."*[31]

Another way Artisans organize is through what we now see as "flash mobs". Instantaneous organizations assembled for whatever purpose when social interaction is needed right now in one place. Messages go out on social media and a time and place is noted. At that appointed time, dozens and sometimes hundreds of people who got the message show up—hence the name "flash mob".

Perhaps the most powerful demonstration of this organizing principle has been in the Middle East with the advent of the "Arab Spring". Country after country (Tunisia, Egypt, Libya and Syria in turn) witnessed the power of disfranchised social groups organizing in a new way. Now that the genie is out of the bottle it will be difficult getting it back in. Right now, this might appear as a silly PR stunt, or a reminiscing of the 60's "happening". But the larger story is that people are learning how to harness technology for social organizing purposes. And this leads us to another Artisan organizing principle: Self-organization. Long a central tent of systems theory, Descartes discussed self-organizing systems much earlier in an unpublished work "The World." and Adam Smith, the hero of the free market, addressed Self-organization in his famous idea of the "invisible hand":

> "Self-organization is the process where a structure or pattern appears in a system without a central authority or external element imposing it through planning. This globally coherent pattern appears from the local interaction of the elements that make up the system, thus the organization is achieved in a way that is parallel (all the elements act at the same time) and distributed (no element is a central coordinator)."[32]

Artisans don't need an identified "leader" or central authority to organize them. They have mastered the internal capacity to self-organize at least in the early stages of people forming into groups and then into communities. At the community stage of development, leaders, no doubt, start to merge. Witness Libya.

Finally, all of these emerging paradigms of organization are powered by technology. Cell phones, social media and the vastness of the Internet are enabling a new kind of social organization. Artisans, being on the vanguard of the new and creative, naturally pick up on this long before others do. The pace and density of human interaction has been increasing throughout history and has taken a quantum leap since the 15th century and the invention of the printing press.

Artisans get their news information via the Internet. They make extensive use of social media sites for connecting with their peers; they seem to have iPhones, Blackberry's and ipads attached to their bodies.[33] Simply put, the technology allows very low cost, instant connectivity with a group or community you can self-define. Perhaps the day of effective mass media has passed us by.

It is now a business maxim that if you want to reach a niche group—especially the younger demographic, aside from brand, your social media strategy is the most important part of your business plan. The technology drops the cost of customer acquisition from dollars to pennies.

I also find it interesting that as the cost of bandwidth decreases more robust mediums are gaining ground. You might call this the YouTube phenomenon. If you don't have an on-line video resume, advertisement or backgrounder you don't belong to the Artisan community.

In conclusion, Artisans organize themselves with new principles and maximize the advantage of technology to give them quick, cheap and robust connections to those they consider their peers. You can see a logical progression of the density of their social networks. They move from small self-organized "groups" to special purpose focused "mobs," and finally forming loose confederations or guilds. You need to understand these organizational principles if you want to connect with the future workers.

How do they act upon the world?

Making these ideas live and breathe seems to be missing today. Politicians have lots of ideas but can't act. Our sacred institutions like education know what needs to be done, but nothing happens. Artisans are important because they are self-organizing and make things happen.

Artisans operate from a set of shared beliefs about the world, and their responsibility for being stewards of the environment. Their major shared belief is about Sustainability, with a capital "S". Artisans are motivated to work with (and maybe for) and live among others who have a similar set of worldviews and expectations. Editorial brevity constrains discussion of what these values are. Suffice to say,

> *"Human sustainability interfaces with economics through the social and ecological consequences of economic activity. Moving towards sustainability is also a social challenge that entails, among other*

factors, international and national law, urban planning and transport, local and individual lifestyles and ethical consumerism. Ways of living more sustainably can take many forms from reorganizing living conditions (e.g., eco-villages, eco-municipalities and sustainable cities), to reappraising work practices (e.g., using permaculture, green building, sustainable agriculture), or developing new technologies that reduce the consumption of resources."[34]

This description is the defining set of shared beliefs held now and increasingly in the future by the Artisans of Thought. They hold that human nature is inherently good, that knowledge comes from interacting with others and the environment, and a strong sense of the ability to create the future.

How do they act as part of the polity? As Max Weber would say, they are a party unto themselves. Fiercely independent and suspicious of the "old guard" they are a pollster's nightmare come true. They tend to be more engaged with grass roots efforts—especially those manifesting their values. Probably the most recent example of this was the 2008 US presidential campaign where a new Internet based political movement took hold and was arguably responsible for the election outcome.

Meetup.org stormed on the scene in early 2001. A social networking site organized around geographies (i.e., zip codes), it quickly became the WAY to gather with like-minded types in your neighborhood. The Obama campaign grabbed onto it as a way to rapidly organize local groups. Today there are over 9.5 million members, 92,000 local groups in 45,000 cities.

And, they are independent. One could argue many reasons why this is occurring. It appears that a shift in fundamental values is driving political behavior, and Artisans are at the vanguard. From the paragon of industrial capitalism we hear,

> *"This is the new mainstream in American politics, and it's growing among younger voters. More than 40% of college undergraduates identify themselves as independents, according to a summer 2008 survey by Harvard University's Institute of Politics (IOP). "Half of*

young Americans do not identify with traditional party or ideological labels -- they are the new center in American politics," says John Della Volpe of IOP."[35]

This emerging segment of modern post-industrial society also moves with extreme speed. They have absolutely no patience with the pace of change in old social institutions. They operate by a "Rule of Two's".

Table 4-2: Rule of Two's

Here's how much time you have you have	... to
2 minutes	... take action on immediate requests for your attention. If you can't handle it that quickly, then it needs to go to someone, or someplace else!
2 hours	... hold face-to-face meetings. If it takes longer than that, you're not planning!!
2 days	... respond to electronic requests. If you can't get to it by then, you're wasting your time and everyone else's.
2 weeks	... assemble a work team and commit to a plan. If you can't find the right people and the right plan by then, the project will fail.
2 months	... identify a business opportunity and test it with customers. If you can't do it by then, your competition can.
2 years	... nothing at all. If your static plans reach out years into the future, the world will have passed you by long before you get them done.

Finally, Artisans operate upon the world with cleverness. They place high value on being clever—out thinking others, especially those who don't share their views. Quite simply they delight in the unexpected, have a high tolerance for uncertainty and see life as a game to be played.

Artisans are game changers. That's their purpose in life. As the old industrial capital system erodes and crumbles, this group will re-create the world. They are the seeds planted in the soil of community over the past three generations, and they are about to break through.

They are our prophets and hold the destiny of society in their hands. They are the Fourth Turning as winter yields to spring.[36] Artisans of Thought don't think about being Artisans, they just are. Here are three things you need to do to become an Artisan of Thought:

- Take responsibility for your own destiny. Declare yourself to be an Artisan of Thought. Your plan is your personal answer to the five parts of this chapter. Write them down, memorize them and repeat them often.

- Realize you don't need someone else to give you your identity, status or formal license to do what you need to do. You don't need a degree, a certificate or a diploma to be an Artisan.

- Practice, practice, practice your art. Every chance you get, show people what you do, what your passion really is.

In the next Chapter we turn to the question of "How do we do that?" We shift upwards a level of energy into the realm of creativity. It is not enough to know who you are; you need to know HOW to manifest your talents.

The New Workplace – Where work is done and how

The hand represents presence of man, his work and achievements. Recognizes man as a vessel for creative power. In our interpretation it is the PLACE where this creative activity takes place.

Chapter 5 – The New Workplace

The central question for this chapter is "How is work to be done"? So much of the how depends on the where because technology makes the flow of work truly distributed in time and space. The good news is you can work anywhere, anytime. The bad news is you can do it everywhere all the time. However, we are human "beings" not human "doings" so we need a PLACE to be comfortable, relaxed and yet focused. Therefore, we gravitate to places where the intent is to work and where we can unleash our creativity. It is our belief that work will be in closer proximity to where we live and where we normally congregate. In short, we will work in our communities, not some far off office tower. We call these new places "Business Community Centers[SM]" because the objective is to foster creative innovation inside our human communities while also maintaining business focus.

Business Community Centers[SM]: The Next Wave in Workplace Innovation

We have recently witnessed a growing connection between corporate real estate (CRE) functions and community-based economic development. The basic connection isn't new, since economic development agencies have been wooing CRE executives to bring their new facilities to town for decades. However, in talking with people around the country, and indeed around the world, we find the old, outdated industrial model continues to rear its ugly head.

It is time for a new model. We believe that economic development in the coming decade cannot be aimed solely at bringing more industrial operations into a community, nor can it be effective by attracting more "big box" retail stores. The world of work is changing, and to effective in adopting to change, communities must take a radical new look at how they attract and retain jobs.

For example, there is a tremendous shift from muscle power and manual dexterity-based employment to jobs fueled by imagination, creativity, and service skills. For example, in the period from 1994 to 2004, the United States witnessed a 20% decrease in farm worker employment and a 23% decrease in tool and die manufacturing However, we had a 78% increase in financial service sales positions and a 61% increase in entertainment, specifically actors and directors. Job opportunities are migrating to different sectors. The widespread economic downturn of 2006-2010 has warped this trend, but it is clear we are moving into a post-industrial economy.

In this post-industrial economy, he way in which we work is also changing. Organizations are becoming smaller and more diffuse. Consider this - small businesses in the US generate 75% of the new jobs. Continuing this trend means that virtually all future growth in employment will take place in small business firms; those firms with fewer than 100 employees.

What remains to be done now to seize the opportunity inherent in working in smaller, dispersed pods by ***moving work to the worker? Today, workers move to the "workplace;" However,*** the technology exists to move work tasks, products and vast amounts of data to the worker. Witness the continuing trend of "off-shoring" knowledge from the United States. We propose a paradigm shift for thinking about where is performed in the US- move that work to the people who can do the work but they may not want to live or drive to dense, urban areas.

Until recently we lacked the organizational infrastructure to make these changes possible. However, a series of workforce development projects in the US and Canada have demonstrated that distributing work to rural areas where there are concentrations of the unemployed (or underemployed) is economically feasible for all stakeholders. Two programs, the Workforce Innovation in Rural Economic Development (WIRED) project in the US and Calgary's WORKshift program have returned very promising results. How can economic development organizations leverage these opportunities? Glad you asked; several things jump out at us.

First and foremost, economic development professionals and their organizations should add as a part of their mission to educate community leaders about their future economic picture. This means helping local leaders across all sectors identify and explore a range of potential scenarios for the future that goes well beyond a simple extrapolation of what's worked in the past. Facilitating and bringing to a conscious level the impacts of changing to meet and capitalize on future forces and also the impact of not changing to meet these forces is a key skill that can mean the vibrancy or slow decline of the community they serve.

The more promising future story suggests that local success will require managed growth policies, less reliance on industry, tourism, and agriculture, and the ability to embrace and respond to change as a part of their growth strategy.

Economic development professionals must become catalysts for change. To accomplish this, they must actively promote the development of consensus among the many disparate interests and constituencies that inhabit any community.[37] Thus, defining a compelling vision and achieving consensus around that vision within the community is the most important task facing anyone wanting to re-shape their community to make it an engine of growth.

We submit that Business Community Centers[SM] offer a compelling solution to the twin challenges faced by both large organizations and local communities. BCCs provide organizations with low-cost, per-worker infrastructure support. They also enable smaller communities to create low-cost office facilities that to help attract and retain knowledge workers whose capabilities will in turn attract companies and well-paying jobs.

The Business Community Center[SM] Concept

A Business Community Center[SM] (BCC) is both a facility and an organizational concept. While there will be a number of variations on the core business model, we anticipate that most BCCs will be owned and operated locally. BCCs offer a combination of traditional office space leases and part-time access to facilities and services on a membership or pay-as-you-go basis.

The most innovative aspect of the our vision is to operate the BCCs as membership organizations that provide their members with access to workplaces and other office facilities and services on a shared, as-needed basis. The BCC will provide a part-time off-site shared working environment primarily for residents of a local community and its surroundings who are either remote employees of large organizations, self-employed professionals, or small business owners.

People who use BCCs are those who choose not to go to a distant corporate facility one or several days a week, or they are small business owners, sole practitioners, and/or "free agents" who need access to a workplace infrastructure and community on a cost-effective basis.

A BCC could also be used as a temporary site for teams working on special projects and they require team space, co-located offices, and support infrastructure on a temporary, time-limited basis. In contrast to what is offered by traditional office leasing and rental organizations, BCC members would pay for space and services only as they need and use them (with a small base-level monthly fee to maintain membership).

This business model produces much lower costs for individual members, yet ensures high usage of the space that in turn provides equity investors and lenders with profitable returns on their real estate and facilities investments.

A Business Community Center^{SM} provides its members with a variety of technologically advanced amenities such as conference rooms, workstations, IT technical support, wireless broadband Internet connectivity, back office administrative support, and informal café-type facilities – all in an ergonomically designed environment. In addition to the technological amenities, many

BBCs are complemented by on-site professional development and business development activities and support.

For larger organizations and growing companies, BCCs provide their employees with all the support services they require on a variable cost basis; thus increasing organizational agility and creating an ability to scale up and down almost instantaneously.

In addition, a BCC will become a community asset, providing meeting space facilities for local educational institutions, public agencies, and other non-governmental organizations. A BCC will serve as a community's "gathering place;" providing local infrastructure with all the amenities normally associated with large organizations and metropolitan areas – at a fraction of the cost.

We expect each BCC to be locally owned and managed, with guidance and consultation (as well as some support services) being provided by a national management company. The role of the management company will be to promote and guide the development of individual BCCs, to provide ongoing infrastructure services, and to foster information exchange across the local units. Thus, local BCC managers and members have access to a national pool of experts and infrastructure services.

The Opportunity

We believe demand for these new kinds of workplaces will rise over the next several years for a number of reasons:

- ♦ Remote and mobile corporate employees do not have adequate alternative meeting places, office services, or technical support that are affordable or convenient to their residential locations

- ♦ Organizations want to move away from a fixed-cost structure to variable cost models to increase their agility and responsiveness to changing environments, while also reducing capital requirements and risk.

- Home-based independent workers also need and want more support and services, because their home-based workspaces are limited and they generally have almost no useful meeting space. And, like mobile workers, they also need office and technical support services that are not readily available in their current situation

Existing workspace offerings typically do not deliver everything that is needed at one location. For example, a remote or independent worker typically travels to a variety of different places like Kinko's, Staples, the UPS store, Starbucks, hotel conference rooms, and so on for supplies and space.

Several other important factors bode well for the success of the Business Community Center^{SM} concept:

- The proliferation of portable technology and work tasks has made remote and mobile work a daily reality for millions of modern workers. This trend is clearly accelerating

- The Internet has become a global infrastructure for information storage, access, and communications; this makes distributed work more the norm than the exception today

- The rising cost of energy and increasing concerns about global warming and other environmental challenges, place increasing pressure on both individuals and communities to reduce traffic congestion and commute times

- Labor-market trends favor the emergence of flexible and individually customized work alternatives

Toward an Organizational Strategy of Place(s)

The events of September 11, 2001, and those that followed in quick succession, made it clear that business operations located in the continental United States cannot count on a stable political environment safe from terrorist attacks. In fact, our new sensitivity to terrorism has also made us much more aware of other factors that threaten business continuity: natural disasters like fires, earthquakes, and hurricanes; regional economic downturns; reliable sources of water and power; changes in local and state government taxation practices; zoning changes; and many more. Strategic real estate decision-making in the future must address three core questions:

1. *Where is the talent?*

    What kind of talent do you need today, tomorrow, and in five years? Where does that talent *want* to live and work? Are there universities and colleges in those locales that will be able to provide you with an ongoing stream of talent? What kind of community amenities are there that will be attractive to your targeted talent pool?

2. *Where is the technology support?*

    You will have more work places than you used to have. All of them must be connected both within the local community and across geographic regions. Reliable high-speed Internet access is an absolute must. So is DSL, Cable, or equivalent access in residential areas so that home-based workers can connect easily to corporate facilities and data.

3. *Where is the multiple location(s) opportunity?*

    Which communities provide you and your workforce with an opportunity to connect central offices, home offices, and third places most efficiently? The quality and extent of the existing transportation infrastructure is a good indicator, since third places are often clustered around transportation nodes. Metropolitan areas with poor public transportation systems would rate lower as candidate locations.

What does all this mean for business success? Knowledge is clearly the primary source of competitive advantage, and knowledge workers drive business success. Yet most companies are not managing knowledge workers effectively. They don't provide workplaces, working conditions, or technology support to meet the wants and needs of their most critical resource. Our research suggests that the costs of the support they do provide are typically 40% –50% higher than they should be.

We believe that a network of over 600 of these new work environments will spring up in the United States in the next five years. The new Business Community Centers™ will enable significant creation of new employment opportunities in communities now hampered with under-utilized real estate, transportation challenges, and a suboptimal quality of life. So, what's the rationale for these "new places of working"?

The Business Case

The major challenges address by these BCC's are pretty straight forward as we have alluded to. Corporations want to move away from fixed costs to more variable cost models that reduce capital requirements and risk while increasing agility. Remote and mobile workers lack adequate meeting alternatives, office services, and technical support. Home-based independent workers need/want more support and services, work space, useful meeting space, office services and technical support. Finally, because xisting offerings do not deliver all that is needed at one location, workers waste a lot of time and resources getting the supplies and space they need to perform their work..

How do the BCCs make money? Some employ a 'Health club' model for basic monthly membership revenue. For example, 350 'members at $150/month 2 days a week access. And, 60% of revenue from additional services such as:

- Tech support
- Admin services and virtual assistants
- Video conferencing
- Business support

Strategically they will become part of national franchise that links the national talent pool to the global market for labor. Eventually, they will also partner with goods and sercice providers who are seeking new distribution channels to these talented workers. Everything from technology (like cell phones and computers) to services such as financial management, preventive health care, insurance and the game chager—education and 'up skilling[38].'

How are they different than current offerings such as "executive suites?" We think there are three major points.

First, significantly lower price. A low monthly membership fee for access modeled after a health club's base membership fee plus incremental charges for incremental uses service fees.

Second, Location with a network of smaller facilities located in or near residential neighborhoods and other needed services and retail outlets. For example: day care and health clubs that leverage under-utilized commercial properties.

Lastly, the experience of the locations has added design elements. They are multi-function (work, learning, service); build on a hospitality interior design model and the coolness factor; a place "where you want to be."

Branding

To summarize and reiterate, we believe our Business Community Center[SM] design concept is unique and readily distinguishable from other "temporary office" and Executive Suite solutions provided by firms like Regus (www.regus.com). The BCC concept includes open, shared "touchdown" workstations as well as closed offices, conference rooms, and other traditional office facilities on a much lower-cost basis. To highlight these differences we have prepared a "strategy canvas" based on ideas described in the book *Blue Ocean Strategy*.

5-1: Blue Ocean Strategy Canvas for the BCC Network

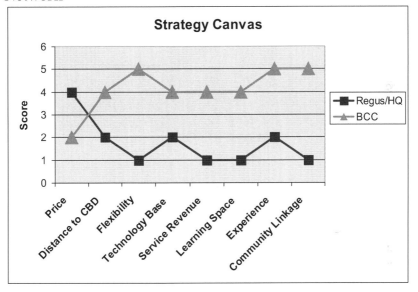

Dimensions of the Canvas:

Price – Cost of membership and/or access. Our cost is a combined low initial fixed-price membership for access, with additional costs based on actual usage.

Distance to CBD – Our locations tend to be further from the Central Business District (of a major metropolitan area), thereby reducing commute time for members. These locations also typically reduce parking costs.

Flexibility – Our hallmark is flexibility of space, depending on current needs. Members can use a small office one day, a touchdown space the next, and different conference room configurations as needed.

Technology Base – Our technology base is a pure Internet play relying on Virtual Private Networks to connect to proprietary servers. Internal technology is secure wireless, with WiMax for wider reach in suburban and exurban areas.

Service Revenue – Our business model envisions at least of 40% of revenues being generated eventually through services such as technology support, administrative services, and discount purchases on other support offerings (e.g., Tech Support, video conferencing, etc.).

Learning Space – Our business model explicitly incorporates on-site and distance learning opportunities in partnership with local educational institutions to support the competency development of BCC members. In addition, the BCC Learning Spaces will be available to local civic and nonprofit groups on a free or highly discounted basis to build good will and support development in the local community.

Experience –The "look and feel" of the workplace. BCC's are designed to be more residential in nature and in particular to foster an experience of community and connectedness.

Community Linkage – BCC's are a center of community work and learning. Unused space (and in particular the Learning Center) can be leased at a nominal rate to local civic groups and non-profits. BCC's are designed to be the new "town square" and/or town hall, following "New Urbanism" principles.

The Future

Communities have choices. We are strongly suggesting that they need to work on building infrastructure that will balance the employment equation such as:

- Education

- Telecommunications
- Affordable housing
- "Places" that work
- Air service

There is a MAJOR shift in the traditional model of institutions that supported the industrial revolution. In our opinion, organizations and communities have two years maximum to make a move and get ahead of the curve – or they face falling behind and losing to the communities who are early adopters.

Putting the Center Back in Community

The BCC is more than just PLACE; it has a culture, management focus, technology AND a relevant physical placement. If we reverse Business Community Centers^{SM} then we need to consider these other parameters.

In the next three chapters we will build on the Business Community Center^{SM} model. BCC's become the new "guild hall" (Chapter 6)--culture. They are the location where our idea of a Talent Integration Ecosystem—management focus-- comes into being (Chapter 7). In our parlance and the language of the future, technology is more about process than anything else. Therefore, BCC's align with the process of becoming; which we discuss in detail in Chapter 8. Keep this in mind as you go through the next three conversations in Chapters 6, 7, and 8. They are parts and pieces that align with the emerging physical structure of work, the Business Community Center^{SM}.

The New Community – How you will live and work together

Eye of the medicine man. A symbol of wisdom and awareness. Where does it come from—in our view it comes from the learning community, the new guild. This is where the medicine man lives.

Chapter 6 – New Communities: The Rebirth of Guilds

We have moved from the question of "what is happening?" to "what skills do I need?" through "what does it look like?" The central question "How is it perceived or seen?" is about self-reflection and using our intuition and imagination. It is about the form of social organization, which can nurture and support the new person as described in chapters 2 through 5.

We suggest that the emergent social form is actually a back-to-the-future scenario. In this chapter we will review the history of guilds and the modern forces driving their re-emergence That is, the failure of industrial institutions, the emergence of technology that speeds up learning, a search for intimate community and the de-evolution of power from the central state. Further, the need for social change is discussed along with a prescription of the functions these new guilds can perform, and those they cannot.

A Brief History

Guilds, as a form of social organization for artisans emerged in Europe in the 13th Century; this is about the same time universities were born. Guilds originated as a way to provide social support to skilled workers so the economic forces would not exploit them, and to protect their "secret knowledge." There remains some argument today as to whether the guilds central purpose was social (protection and networking) or economic (market protection and exclusion).[39]

Guilds have a long history. There is some evidence that they existed in some form as craft associations dating back to the 3rd Century BC in the Roman Empire and likewise in the Han dynasty. Wherever specialized skills and knowledge arose, these associations formed to focus and organize the practice of their craft. Guilds fell from grace and usefulness as the Industrial Revolution took hold in the 19th Century. In a sense, they were replaced by labor unions and cartels.

In retrospect, and in terms of today's language, you could say Guilds existed to protect and pass on intellectual property created before we had patents, copyrights and associated legal systems. They related to the larger economy, as they were places where young people went to learn a trade, find work and a supportive social network. From Guilds emerged apprenticeships, journeymen and masters of craft. As you saw earlier, these basic needs have not changed; new forces are driving our modern "artisans of thought"[40] back to answering a basic need.

Industrialization and capitalism supplanted the needs for guilds through concurrent development of public education, work specialization and routinization of work tasks. Guilds began to lose influence and disappear as a philosophy of "free trade" and laissez-faire economic theory moved to the forefront. Karl Marx criticized guilds for their rigid social structure.[41]

Degrees replaced certifications of "masterpieces" and time in class, as measured by "credits," replaced long apprenticeships. Interestingly, mass industrialization also did away with specific towns being known for the type of work done there as factories spread to locations closest to sources of power and raw material—instead of knowledge. A trend, we would suggest is turning around.

Currently, guilds exist, albeit in diminished form, as the Screen Actors Guild and National Association of Realtors, and legal bar associations in the United States. Above all, in today's world, consultants behave very much like the journeyman of old. Travelling, spreading ideas, and working with a number of different clients. Most recently we note that online computer gamers have begun to form "players guilds."[42]

Driving Forces

Several social forces are driving the rebirth of guilds as a way of organizing talent pools. While there are a myriad of social, economic and political pressures on the 21st Century global economy, we feel four are of particular interest for the re-emergence of guilds.

Failure of industrial institutions

After a nearly 500-year lapse, we are seeing fundamental changes in society once again. For example, the printing press was the primary cause of this transformation in the late 15th century. While fantastic inventions and technologies have come along since then, nothing else has come close until the invention of the Internet. As we head into the 21st century, the Internet is prompting social change of the same nature and magnitude as the printing press (Bressler and Grantham, 2000).

Without a doubt, the institutions that served humanity well in the industrial era have reached the end of their useful life. Just as feudalism fell away with the Age of Enlightenment and royalty fell with the rise of the modern nation-state, so in addition, industrial capitalism, tribal governments and supporting establishments are falling away.

Technology speeds up education and continuous learning

The invention and diffusion of radical technology inevitably changes how we live, work, and learn together as a human race. Technology, especially when it influences how we *communicate* with each other, causes a change in our sense and experience *of time and space*. This, in turn, brings about a change in our *mental energy* or how we pay attention to things, and finally in *our behavior* and how we interact with the world.

While the Internet is changing how businesses and customers connect with each other, none of this comes close to matching the broader human changes we are beginning to see. Consider how our world changed after the introduction of Johan Gutenberg's printing press. From E-learning to the Occupy Wall Street movement, a Fourth Turning is emerging in our global society.

Search for community that is intimate

It is hard to argue against a growing desire for community around the planet. The Arab Spring, ascendency of an Asian superpower, crisis in the European "Union," and political gridlock in the United States, all have at their root a renewed desire to work together in community—not against each other in power struggles.

Historically, in the West at least, small villages and towns traditionally centered community structures near a parish church and one or two eating establishments. Here people would gather to be with one another and exchange ideas and information. With the concurrent rise of mercantilism, the wealth that was created in these rural areas was sucked into the larger urban areas where wealth focused on the construction of these large structures and monuments.

The basic unit of social organization, and hence community, was organized by the church. However, the church's penetration into every aspect of community life was not complete. Community based on tradition and celebrated events signified the rhythms of agricultural life.

Community was important to people as they entered the industrial age. Community was the social glue that held everything together, gave people hope, and provided them with a psychological anchor in times of trouble. In addition, this is where we are today. Just as the world was getting bigger and people felt connected to a broader world, community became much more local and amorphous than it had been when it was decreed from some central authority. Indeed history does repeat itself.

Devolution of power

We contend that political power is devolving from massively centralized structures to a loosely knit network of community federations. During the Middle Ages, government and religion were intertwined. One could not easily separate the two. It depended on the area of the world in which you lived as to which of these two basic social structures had primacy in your everyday life.

The sub-plot of this story is that the printing press had a major impact on society that continues to today. That is, government and religion separated and each regulated our lives in different ways. The function of both involves the influence and regulation of behavior in terms of what people can and cannot do. Underlying all of this regulation and control lies a belief system that is agreed-upon and shared. So when belief structures change, eventually so does the governance structure. At this point in our history, beliefs are changing once again; with changed beliefs will be a change in Government.

The change in government structure in the Middle Ages, was generally a move from a feudal form to empires and nation states. Society began to organize itself around shared beliefs, fears, values, and desires as a group that was significantly larger than what they had been able to experience directly in one day's travel time. The underlying value shift that occurred was that people went from protecting the territory and resources surrounding them to focusing on upholding their beliefs and controlling what mattered most to them. People went from standing at the gates to ward off invaders, to looking further out; hoping their common culture could grow in size. Today, a similar change is occurring as summarized in Table 6-1.

Table 6-1: Printing Press vs. Internet

	Printing Press	Internet
Technology	Oral to print	Analog to digital
Time/Space Perception	History to present	Present to future
Mental Energy	Automatic to conscious	Conscious to intentional
Behavior	Reactive to ego	Ego to purpose

What type of government will emerge that supports purpose driven behavior; intentional action for the larger good; a future orientation and more symbolic communication? We do not quite know yet; but it will be vastly different from our collective experience over the past 500 years

Social Change

The basic structure of work behavior is changing. Our society (at least the developed world) is moving away from an industrial model to a community-based model that strangely resembled how we organized ourselves—before the Industrial Revolution. So, it's back to the future of work. These medieval work organizations were called guilds and they were a central fact of economic life for centuries.

Specially organized groups known as guilds exercised control of economic life in the Middle Ages. The essential purpose of guilds was to create monopolies. They tried to exclude from the local market so far as possible, both the outside trader and the local independent trader who was not a member of the guild. Their social attitude was to some extent influenced by the church, but their aim was to use the town market peacefully, profitably, and pleasantly for themselves alone[43].

A research group at MIT conducted a broad sweeping analysis of future trends of work in late 2003[44]. One of the key features they saw emerging was the re-emergence of guilds to help organize and protect those workers we have discussing.

These early organizations represent only a beginning. If flexible working arrangements of various sorts become even more common in the future, we will need much more extensive ways of meeting the human needs of the individuals who work in them. It is common, in our industrial age mindset, to assume that meeting these needs is the responsibility of the employer, the government, or the individuals themselves.

What Guilds Could Do

What if there was a new kind of organization, whose purpose was not to produce any specific product, but to meet the emerging and unmet needs of its members? These guilds could provide a stable home for their members as they moved from job to job. They could, for example, help their members by:

- ❖ Ensuring their financial security

- ❖ Providing placement and professional training services, and

- ❖ Becoming a locus of social interaction and identification

Guilds appear to be an especially promising way of addressing two challenges. First, by providing insurance and pensions; professional development and placement programs; and access to a social milieu, guilds can allow workers to take advantage of flexible employment relationships. In addition, they offer the potential for greater productivity without having to face high risks and unattractive social repercussions.

Second, by emphasizing continuous learning for their members and the matching of workers' skills with available opportunities, the interests of guilds will be closely aligned with those of the companies for which the guilds' members will work.

This new approach has the potential to radically change the terms of debates that have been central to the industrial age. Today, for instance, collective bargaining is a primary role of many unions; we typically assume the interests of unions and management will be in conflict. However, in a world of flexible networks of one-person companies, unions do not have is a stable centralized management with which to bargain. An attractive future opportunity for unions; therefore, is to move toward fulfilling the needs of their members in the guild-like ways as described. We foresee opportunities for many kinds of organizations including professional societies, unions, neighborhoods, colleges, churches, and others to be creative and proactive in meeting needs that are likely to become increasingly urgent as flexible working arrangements become more common.

At the same time, guilds cannot magically provide better pay or benefits for workers who lack skills or bargaining power. For the same reasons that unskilled workers are not attractive job candidates, they will also be unattractive candidates for joining guilds. However, in guilds based on shared interests such as family ties, place of residence, or religious beliefs, economic considerations will be less important in determining who can join.

Ownership of the Means of Preservation

A return to guilds as an organizing force for the worker of the future will bring with it another medieval institution: a return of ownership of means of production to the individual. In our surveys of distributed workers over the years, we have noted a consistent finding. Workers report that the technology they have in their home offices is more advanced and sophisticated than what their employers provide in the central office.

In fact, many report that they 'save the toughest jobs for home' because they have better tools. As technology has become commoditized, individuals can afford to own the fastest, latest and most robust equipment. No longer, must a worker depend on his employer to give him/her the tools they need to do their job; they have their own. So, if artisans have their own telecommunications, computers, databases, cell phones and meeting places, what do they need in terms of infrastructure from an 'employer?'

Expecting workers to bring their own tools to the job could radically re-shape how corporations look at the management of hard assets. Why should they purchase and maintain them, when perhaps 30% of the workforce has their own?

The return to guilds, as a way of organizing work communities, has tremendous implications for the provision of services to workers. In the old industrial model, companies provide workers with everything they need to do the job: office space, technology, and management support; and they provide health care, pensions and training. However, guilds also provide all that for workers.

Talent Integration Ecosystems

Therefore, if our scenario plays out, then companies will find themselves in the envious position of shedding the responsibility of providing human resource services, technology infrastructure and facilities. Think of the impact this could have. You could literally cut your operational expenses in half for 30-40% of the workforce. All this and community too! But wait, what's the dark side for companies and what will they have to do to counteract loosening their social ties with workers?

In short, their death. Loosening community ties implies a growing lack of engagement between worker and company. Companies have historically existed to find, organize and focus the energy and talent of people who add value through innovation, manufacture and distribution of goods and services. Some form of human organization will be required to step in and fill that gap. As we have suggested above, that organization we believe will be a re-birth of guild structures. Just what will that look like? It's hard to say at this writing. The closest we can envision is something like the "Occupy" movement spreading across the planet. We prefer to focus on what it will do to fill the void, instead of what it will look like. We suggest thinking of a Talent Integration Ecosystem (TIE) (More about this in the next chapter). We think TIEs will perform eight functions that companies and large formal organizations performed during the Industrial era. TIEs will be the social psychological engine of value creation in the future.

- Purpose finding

This is the function of helping people find their true purpose. Almost a spiritual activity, purpose finding is about answering the age-old human condition questions: "Why I am here; what am I supposed to do?" It is our contention that TIEs will step up and be the Community that guides, coaches and provides support to people on their journey towards living out purpose.

- Strengths analysis

Instead of approaching human development from a perspective of "deficit reduction," TIE guilds will assist people in coming from a position of individual strength. "What do you do best?" "What can you do better than others?" There are many pathways towards this end. TIEs will be the place where people can get the tools, analytical frameworks and methods to find their strengths.

- Motivation

The next step up the ladder toward the vision of potential is motivation. What is my passion? What do you feel "called" to do? Each person has a different set of motivations. Understanding these is a key to success and a feeling of fulfillment. Sorting out needs from wants will be central to moving from a society characterized by consumerism to one of collaborative intention.

- Futures Search

How does one get to this personal end state? Our belief is that you have to be eternally vigilant, constantly scanning the environment for signals of change. It short, how does one become ultimately flexible and agile? You need to establish a sensing capability that reaches out, pulls in information, sorts it, sifts it and continuously re-paints a picture of the future. Searching the future horizon is the basic input to directed change. There are many ways of doing this. People can be taught techniques of future searching, but first they need to be motivated to spend the time and energy doing this.

- Education and competencies

TIEs will augment and at times replace our traditional education system. Enabled by technology that allows people separated in time and space to learn together. These social learning systems operate by developing "competencies", not skills. The lines between learning and working will disappear. They will become blended. Certificates of service (which we call degrees and resumes) will no longer be enough to place people in an innovation economy where they can contribute their maximum. Again tightly coupled social guilds will become the mechanism.

- Internships

We think that that actual mechanism for doing these things will look much more like internships where doing and being are combined on a day-to-day basis. Time spent under the tutelage of "masters of the craft" will be the answer to "how to do it. We spoke elsewhere of the emergence of "artisans of thought" as a detailed picture of this process. You become an artisan of thought through a process of internship—again guided along the way by a TIE.

- Mentoring

On the other side of this equation is the process of mentoring, or coaching. The guides will be the older members of society whose purpose is to pass on the wisdom and knowledge amassed over a lifetime. But there has to be a linkage between mentors and mentees. It used to be done on a haphazard fashion in our universities and companies. A new way of building these social networks is emerging.

- Continuous learning

The last step in this process will be continuously learning. Much has been said about this topic in the past few decades, but most of the talk has been about skills and discrete abilities. We see the need in a much broader context. Skills yes, but also continuous learning about intellectual, social and spiritual capacities.

So. There you have it. The emergent social form of the 21st Century for Artisans of Thought will be guilds. Guilds will serve the function that higher education and professional organizations performed. Purpose driven people, or Artisans of Thought, have new sets of competencies and they form into guilds. Next, we tackle the issue of integrating who we are with what we do.

Doing, Being, Thriving – Connecting with something bigger than you

The medicine wheel, or circle of life. A physical manifestation of spiritual energy. A bringing together of all the pieces needed to give breathe to life and sustain it.

Chapter 7 – Being, Doing and Living

The basic question posed in this chapter is: "How can we understand what needs to be done?" This chapter is about integrating who we are, what we do and how to live this out. It is about connecting with something larger than us. Just as Chapter 2 was about our individual purpose, this chapter completes the path and deals with connecting and integrating that purpose with something at a higher level. It is about self-knowledge and getting rid of attachments to things and greed.

Knowing

This chapter really has two basic parts. The first part is about how to bring all that information and advice from the first six chapters and make it real. We call this process the ***Talent Integration Ecosystem*^{sm}**. It is a method to do what we've been talking about for 150 odd pages. It is the **place**, process, **and** all that we have discussed.

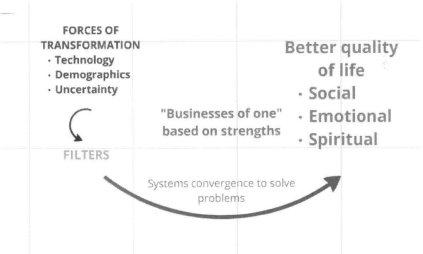

The remainder of the chapter is aimed at a deeper level, the more spiritual: bringing being, doing and living together. The second part of this chapter is the bridge to the next one where we do a deep dive on personal transformation. Bear with us as we set the stage.

Weaving the Social Fabric of 21st Century Communities

There are many threads weaving together in this world of the future. As we have alluded to, it is a rebirth of social organizations called guilds. We also contend that these new guilds will organize in a new and modern way via Talent Integration Ecosystem^{SM}. This discussion itself could (and should) be a long one. Here, we just want to give you an overview to engage your thinking.

The purpose of these new guilds is to develop local talent in a way that meets the needs of citizens, commerce and communities while fostering sustainability. They will add value to our communities by:

1. Produce a continuously adaptive system and sustainable talent pool. Things won't stand still so these ecosystems have to have an inherent capability to keep moving, changing and evolving. And that means always spending time, money and energy looking to the future.

2. Increase community well-being so that the community becomes a magnet for talent. Not only do you want to keep your homegrown talent in the community, but you also want to make it extremely attractive for others to move there.

3. Create a unique identity. This is community brand management. What is unique that makes people proud to say that's where they live and work? You know you have a unique identity when people start printing the community's name and identity on T-shirts and baseball caps.

Elements of the System

A number of organizations and entities with shared needs come together around a common purpose to collaborate on solutions that benefit the community. These are the base elements of your ecosystem. And this is where it gets difficult. A number of the old institutions are dying because they have lost their relevance to the emerging world. So, it's hard to talk about something that is needed when we don't have words for the components. We prefer to use a metaphor from chemistry and call them atoms and molecules. You need certain kinds of atoms to combine and make a talent integration ecosystem molecule.

- o A learning atom. Traditionally these have been high schools, colleges and universities. Not anymore. Teachers, mentors and learners connected by technology. It needs visibility and a place for people to connect.

- o Social service atoms. This is the "Heart" of the community. Usually civic groups, faith based organizations and self-help organizations. They are now becoming self-organized groups with limited half-lives. They come and go, but the leaders usually move from one issue to another as the evolving need dictates.

- o An expressive atom. The arts and culture part of your community. If you don't have an active one, you are dead. This is the soul of your ecosystem. Art in all its forms (performing, visual and emerging media) serves to satisfy a basic human instinct for harmony, balance, and rhythm. It communicates the experience of mystery in the community.

- o A structural atom. This is the atom, which puts in place, and maintains a persistent pattern of interaction among and between community members. Usually seen as micro-social units of neighborhoods and/or ethnic based organizations. Today we call them "grass roots" groups.

- o A regenerative atom. This is the "sustainable" component. It serves the function of preserving the physical environment including critical resources such as air, water, and land. We like to think of this as the part that can provide the necessities of human life without a heavy dependence on external resources.

Action focus areas

Once you have these "atoms" in place in the talent integration ecosystem they need to do something. What's their functional purpose? We believe this ecosystem has five basic functions to perform.

- ❖ Promotion of citizen involvement—everyone in the community needs to be involved. This is the reach out find the resources you need within the community. If it isn't there right now, how do you go back and rely on the "learning atom" to produce the talent you need? It takes a great deal of involvement. Without this involvement and commitment the systems stagnates.

- ❖ Job creation through entrepreneurial projects—creation and innovation are the key processes. Central to any community is an economic activity that produces more wealth (economic, social and spiritual) than it consumes. We are suggesting that this takes a post-industrial form of "business of one"—or at least a very few. Call them "micro-businesses," but grow WITHIN the community.

- ❖ Purpose finding for people—you can't get there without truly knowing why you are on the journey. This function is often overlooked. Finding purpose is a personal journey now. No longer does a family, a church, or a school give your purpose to you. Your personal journey now is finding your calling and learning how to live out that calling within the context of your local community.

- ❖ Organizational leadership development—new competencies will be needed by those who lead the process. We see "gaming" as a metaphor for organizations coming forward. And leaders in the gaming world are quite a bit different than traditional leaders. It is multi-generational, cross gender and multidisciplinary in thinking.

- ❖ Fundraising for local facilities—the financial and emotional resources needed for this process should come from the community itself. This will be the key to sustainability. The talent integration ecosystem must produce wealth in excess of what it needs to survive. It can either re-invest this excess into local capacity building, or export a portion in exchange for other goods and services.

How do you build a new guild?

As we have said before, the fundamental activity of the guild is building increased social capital capacity inside the community. One of the core principles is that people in the community need to be the central actors in this process. Outside resources merely provide ideas, tools and connections. Local citizens accomplish the work itself. We think there are six major sets of competencies, which are required. These competencies make up the "curriculum" for the learning atom if you will. Several areas are addressed simultaneously:

- ❖ Communications skills—learning how to listen, talk to each other and engage in civil dialog

- ❖ Meeting management—how to help and facilitate group decision-making

- ❖ Community organizing—how to be inclusive in your community social engagement management

- ❖ Entrepreneurship—what it really means to be creative, independent and free of history in your economic activities

- ❖ Leadership development—continuously and consciously creating more leadership capability and knowing how and when to shift these responsibilities given the needs of the moment

- ❖ Adaptive Planning—always looking forward. Having people who are scouts to the future and visionary in the long term

What does it look like?

Here's a word picture of what this looks like when it's working.

Measures of Success

It's often said that you can't measure it, you can't manage it. We prefer a slightly different metaphor of flying an airplane. You need to know your direction, your altitude and your speed to do basic navigation of getting from where you are to where you want to go. For us direction translates into an economic development program; altitude is your community experience factors; and speed is the amount of direct service your talent integration ecosystem provides. In sum:

Economic Development	Community Experience	Direct Service
Job growth	Social diversity	Number of workshops hosted
Population change	Performing Arts support	
Ecosystem quality	Civic involvement	Number of participants
Education level	Social action programs	Number of business plans authored
Crime rates	Recreational variety and access	Number of businesses in operational at 24 month timeframe
Housing affordability		
Health care access	Level of faith based organizational involvement	

Examples of it working

When we begin to discuss these ideas, people always ask for examples. Listed below are "guild" based T.I.E. communities we are working with to bring forth the vision:

- ❖ Past
  - ➢ Hagenberg, Austria (http://en.wikipedia.org/wiki/Softwarepark_Hagenberg)
  - ➢ Jamtland, Sweden (http://en.wikipedia.org/wiki/J%C3%A4mtland)
- ❖ Present
  - ➢ Dexter Neighborhood, Prescott, AZ
  - ➢ Western Region, MI (http://www.wiredwestmi.org/)
- ❖ Future
  - ➢ Mesa del Sol, Albuquerque, NM (http://mesadelsolnm.com/)

We have included a tactical "playbook" for you to use. You'll find it in the final chapter on resources. Let's take this discussion of being, doing and living up a level. We covered the living and doing; now let us move to the being part of the equation.

The Spiritual Dimension of Systemic Change

"You've got to be careful if you don't know where you are going, because you might not get there" - Yogi Berra

The Back-story

Four business people sitting around a gracious dinner table discussing how to design work environments of the future that will offer people an opportunity to better balance work activity and the rest of their lives.[45] All of a sudden, the conversation turns to spirituality in the workplace. Serendipity (i.e., to make discoveries, by accident and sagacity, of things not in quest of) has struck again. So here we have a Roman Catholic, an evangelical, agnostic and a Buddhist talking the same thing. This deserves attention.

The Plot

It goes without saying that the world of work is changing very quickly these days. The on-rush of technology, globalization of markets, emerging new models of business, and some of the most dramatic changes in demographics in decades have all combined to form the perfect storm for organizational change. Loss of connection, meaning, place and identity are the headlines in our lives. The pace of change is perhaps, more dramatic than humans have seen in 500 years.

Those of you who have followed our work over the past few years have heard this chant before. Drucker's predictions of the demise of large formal corporations (Will the Corporation Survive?", *The Economist*, November 1, 2001); Strauss and Howe's prognostications of the 'fourth turning' (http://www.fourthturning.com/) and countless others who see radical, significant changes in both the process and structure of how we organize our lives to work, play, learn and commune.

An awakening seems to be occurring.

The Antagonists

At the same time, the professions we would think would be gearing up to help with the birth of these new social forms, seem to be strangely quiet. For example, we notice that one preeminent human resources management professional association hasn't had a seminar or discussion session on the 'future of work' for at least three years.

Others focused almost exclusively on change management appear to be stuck somewhere in 1968 T-group psychology. But these observations are not meant to malign those groups of professionals, but to point to the fact that something is missing. And we obviously have an idea of what that missing ingredient is. But first let's step back and look at what organizational change is all about and why it's so important.

The Protagonist

Change upsets people. It upsets them for a number of reasons. But at the heart of it, change does three psychological things:

- It causes a temporary loss of identity
- It changes our social status within our peer group and community
- It creates a shift in power relationships among members of our social network

Industrial society focused us on answering a fundamental metaphysical question (**Who am I?**) in terms of our relationship to our livelihood. The classical social theorists like Weber, Marx and Durkheim quite adequately explained these dynamics. However, the point is, individuals have linked their identity to their job title, the company they work for, and perhaps over the past 20 years to their profession. Who they are has become what they do! And this identity issue runs counter to human nature—more about that in a minute.

Again, our status is largely determined by the work we do and, more to the point, by the money we make doing that work. The symbols of status are everywhere. Some lust after the salary so they can possess the symbols. In today's world that means SUV's, McMansions, gated communities, boats and now even 'toy haulers' to carry everything around in. We tend to inexplicably tie our **perception of self-worth** is tied inexplicitly to our possessions, which emanate from our employment. People know us by our trappings.

Power is ones' ability to influence or control the behavior of others. Whereas this is somewhat correlated with status is a distinct psychological dimension. An excess or deficit of power has been shown to have very visible effects on our mental states, attitudes and behavior. **For example, our purpose comes into question** during a time of organizational change when people perceive their power to diminish. The external force causes diminished power and results in an outward expression of hostility that serves to diffuse anxiety.[46]

We think one of the major reasons orchestrating successful organizational change is so difficult is that most practitioners approach the problem from a perspective of psychological acceptance, or worst yet, rational economic behavior. What's missing is attention to the spiritual dimension of our lives. Homo sapiens are descendants of tribal animals who have evolved from a rich symbolic environment. We are after all, human **BEINGS**, not human **DOINGS**. And being is the providence of spirituality. Change will only be successful if the spiritual dimension is acknowledged and dealt with![47]

> *"We are not human beings having a spiritual experience. We are spiritual beings having a human experience."*
> *- Tielhard de Chardin*

The Reconciliation

That being the case, what can we do to interject a spiritual dimension, say even practice, into organizational change?[48] Especially when it is occurring in the context of other failing social institutions, from which we have traditionally brought meaning to our lives such as political, educational and religious structures. We are talking here of the spiritual which is not the religious dimension of our lives, although the two are often confused. Spirituality (in our sense here) is more about the personal search for answers and understanding; religion is more of a socially organized effort, or praxis, towards the same end. We believe that within the context of organizational change and its impact on the individual we need a more personal approach—a spiritual one.

Let us start with the basics: Identity. Herein lies a glimmer of hope. Younger generations of workers and those displaced from the industrial workforce do not depend on work relationships for identity as much as some other groups. Nonetheless, it is an issue, the change process must address. We'll save the choice of method for another time, be it training, counseling, mentoring or whatever.

The point here is the outcome of having people find the answer to 'Who am I?' come from somewhere other than their employment. It's a choice we get to make, not something thrust upon us from the outside. We get to create our own reality.[49] We think the answer lies in a process of self-discovery, guided by a new social network made up of persons from other aspects of our lives such as the community, church, family and professional associates. The action required is to consciously re-construct your network with the purpose being to discover your true essence, your spirit.

Status. Giving up the big house, car(s) and boat can be tough. The essence again lies in a change in perspective. If you are outwardly focused (status determined by others) your perception of self-worth comes from others and you internalize it. However, if the focus of self-worth comes from introspection, something changes. You become who you define yourself as. Eastern spiritual traditions place an emphasis on work as service. No matter how menial or lofty, work can (should) become right livelihood in Buddhist terms. If you do what gives you and consequentially others joy, clinging to status will disappear as the apparition it truly is.

> *"Once you make a decision, the universe conspires to make it happen"*
> *- Ralph Waldo Emerson*

Power is about purpose. People who seek power are often confused about their purpose in the world. People who cling to power are afraid they have no purpose.

It may be that this is the core issue facing the increasing irrelevance of modern corporations. Obscene profits, reckless lack of regard to the environment and abuse of power are hallmarks of toxic work environments. So, how do you help people discover their true purpose in the midst of turbulent times?

The first step in the process is recognizing that all organizational change is really about personal change and growth. When a large number of people engage in this process at the same time— organizations change. There are, however, significant personal, individual barriers that have to be overcome. There is fear of change, uncertainty about the outcome and self-doubt about being able to 'do it.' We have to realize that this fear, uncertainty and doubt exist and confront it explicitly, not ignore it nor dismiss its importance to people.

I think it takes extreme personal courage to confront a lifetime of purposelessness. An awakening is required. Every religious tradition has its answer to this question. However, they all come back to the truth that the highest purpose for humans is to serve a larger goal; a goal that that benefits more than just one person. If this higher purpose is lacking in your 'work' your soul is lost. Getting clear on purpose and how to serve that purpose is required to navigate these roiling rapids in the river of change. But take heart there are many paths to enlightenment.

There is an ancient Buddhist koan that goes something like this:

> Student: Master what should one do before enlightenment?
>
> Master: Chop wood, carry water.
>
> Student: Master what should one do after enlightenment?
>
> Master: Chop wood, carry water.

Fade to Black

In conclusion, then we assert that there is something lacking in most efforts towards facilitating organizational change. And we observe that organizational change is occurring with increased rapidity and impact. The missing, critical, ingredient is the spiritual dimension of human change, or evolution. There are many pathways toward enlightenment, each guided by a different tradition—and they are all correct.[50]

- **We see a loss of identity, which can be dealt with by consciously focusing on defining who we are with the help of a re-constructed social network outside of our work**

- **We see a change in status, which can be dealt with through an introspective approach to assessing self-worth**

- **We see a letting lose of power, which can be dealt with by seeking a purpose greater than oneself**

We will not be so bold as to suggest specific ways for people to attain these lofty goals. There are a myriad of traditions, creeds and beliefs. *We simply encourage you to build your own theology in times of change.*

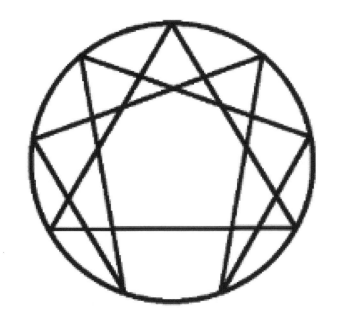

Thriving and Sustaining – Going beyond what you thought possible.

The enneagram. We take it from the tradition of Sufi mysticism brought to us in the works of G. I. Gurdjeiff and J.G. Bennett. It represents a process of continuous coming into being and improvement from one cycle to the next.

Chapter 8 – Thriving and Sustaining

OK the last Chapter of the journey. The main question answered in this chapter is: "What is the conscious connection between a person, their community and their work?" This is about how you can expand your current limits; it is about YOUR transformation. Thriving happens on all levels simultaneously. A person can't thrive in a dead community and communities can't thrive with dead, stagnant individuals. You have to do it all. We know that is a confusing picture and we will do our best to give you a roadmap. First, we begin at the personal level and then move it up to the community and finally commerce.

First Things First

In order to thrive (not just survive) in the future you need to first get on firm ground. Remember back in Chapter 2 we talked about finding your purpose? Well that is all well and good, but it actually goes deeper. Terry has developed a process that gets at this deeper need to become more agile at the personal level. He calls it the 9 Element or 9E® process. We have included a ton of additional resources on 9E® in the resource section. The highlights are here, details later.

The 9E® process is evolutionary and transformational in nature – it is a journey for the rest of your life. Through a facilitated and structured process that raises your awareness of what you already know, you become more satisfied with, engaged in, and fulfilled by the life you choose to live.

This program supports an evolutionary progression to deepening levels of satisfaction, engagement and fulfillment along with the corresponding expansion of Presence; one of the nine (9) Es'. The desired outcome of the 9E® process is peacefulness, which can be described as sustained fulfillment. The intent of peacefulness is to be in a state of present moment awareness where you can experience calmness and serenity, as well as being centered and grounded. For your understanding, below is a short summary of the 9 elements. Another way to view the 9 elements is by the internal and external nature of this work. The first four elements are data heavy and focused internally; that is, on you becoming aware of who you are. When you define your Purpose (element 4), you reach the tipping point in element 5 of the range of possibilities open for you in the external world. The remaining four elements are focused externally on aligning your behavior with who you are. It looks like this:

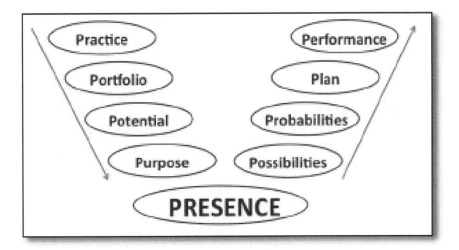

We have included additional material on the 9E® process in the resource chapter if you are interested.

Mastering the Universe

What do you do with this when you have gone through the 9E® process? Now that you have mastered yourself, why not take on the universe? In case you have not noticed, our world is beginning to organize itself without the direction of any central authority. If we had to put a date on it, we'd say the Arab Spring of 2011 marked the visible beginning of self-organization.

Now that this self-organizing movement has spread to the United States in the form of the Occupy Wall Street (aka OWS) phenomenon, we thought a little reflection and an update of the thinking would be helpful as we frame up this new conversation. Maybe we have a"9E®" process going on at the community level. We think so.

We will let our friends at OWS decide at the national level what we want from our government. Our purpose here is to take a deep dive and ask the same question at the local level. First, there is a preamble followed by three parts.

Last Spring planet Earth saw just what an emergent, self-organizing society could look like. The people in Tunisia, Egypt, Libya and perhaps Syria decided their governmental operating system (GOS), the one they have had for more than a generation, did not work anymore. They decided to "uninstall" that system. It is not clear, yet, what new system they will install to replace it. This all reminds us of when we finally gave up on MS-DOS and migrated to a Windows platform. Remember how that felt?

Our point here is that a similar "uninstall" and system migration is called for in local government. The same is probably true at the national level—that's what OWS is really all about. It's not a simple re-boot of the existing system but a clean install. Actually, we see a speed-up of the "de-evolution" of centralized power and provision of services, down to the community level. And that's what I want to talk about. What could that localized community governance look like?

First, we have to realize that the human-computer environment is a platform of connections that speeds up this process. The FAX was instrumental in the disintegration of the old Soviet regime and we have seen Twitter and Facebook power along events in the Middle East. So how do we leverage the "i-Citizen" and "e-Government" movements that have already begun? Did you know what a "meet-up" was five years ago? What will things look like at the ground level in five more years? What political power will be usurped when Facebook meets YouTube?

We see three interrelated features:

1. Smaller, better local government
2. Co-production of services, and
3. Community-based government

Smaller, better government

At some point in growth, administrative systems become sub-optimal. My friend, Duane Elgin describes this as a limit to large organizational systems.[51] We have reached that point of sub-optimization at the State and local levels. We spend more energy on coordinating things, than getting things done. If you don't believe me, go down to City Hall and ask for an explanation of a policy. Cut it down by 35% to start. Start giving people the tools to do things for themselves; do not do it for them.

There are four guiding principles for smaller, better local government. First, it needs to be more effective. By that, I mean local government needs to serve its citizens. It does things that improve their quality of life, sense of engagement with the democratic process and their wellbeing. (http://www.well-beingindex.com/monthlyWBIreport.asp).

Second, local government has to be transparent. Seems apparent doesn't it. Open meeting laws, open participation and everything public. This is not rocket science folks. It's been done for decades in business. It's called "open book management". http://en.wikipedia.org/wiki/Open-book_management. I've done case studies on firms using this transparency and it's amazing, although somewhat painful for the older more entrenched hierarchical interests.

Third, Local government needs be responsive to necessary changes, in other words, more agile. That means breaking out of an annual budget-setting mentality for example. Things like an on-going planning process with quarterly reviews and flexibility (within limits of course) at the department head level.

Lastly, smaller, better government needs to shift from a mindset of providing "product" to citizens to one of providing a "service." They must evolve with the "citizen consumer." The old psychological belief system that "businesses are formed around products" has changed. It has shifted to a belief that "businesses are formed around service." People now expect more than just 'things.' They want to be taught how to use products properly and they want to know how using this product will improve their own work and quality of life. For example, it's not trash collection, but educating citizens on waste management such as re-cycling.

Now, let us consider the "how" of it all.

Co-production of services

We need governance systems that teach people how to do things like energy conservation, environmental protection, learning, job training and yes, preventive health care. People AND government working together. Citizens control the quality and level of service. The protesters in Egypt actually re-built the streets in Tahrir Square after the "uninstall." They didn't wait for the street maintenance department to schedule a capital improvement project.

First, we need a truly collaborative relationship between public and private sectors. I have a feeling this can only happen when the larger OWS movement sorts out who is responsible for what. The fundamental policy question is (as I hinted earlier) what should the public sector really do? And what should they NOT do? Until we answer this question, we cannot get the two sides to collaborate because they both have a different answer to that question. So, there is the first roadblock to co-production of "services" to citizens.

If done correctly, this can lead to quicker delivery of goods and services we need and at a lower cost. Frankly, the high cost of most "services" is due to the rapidly increasing costs of coordination between all the moving parts of the system of delivery. This is the point that Duane Elgin makes when he suggests we are at that limit of efficiency in many institutions. The only solution to that conundrum is to remove the requirement for coordination. Any manager knows that when you push accountability down in a system and cut out intermediate levels things get done quicker and usually with a higher degree of quality. Let people on the ground make decisions. When was the last time you went to a meeting with an elected representative and felt the time you spent was productive?

This leads directly to my last point of citizens co-producing what they need with their governments. Let citizens control the level of service they get and pass judgment on quality. Sure, we do not have mechanisms in place today to do that. However, we have learned a lot from the quality movement and six-sigma about all that could be transferred to communities. Why aren't we doing that? Simply put if we did there would not be a need for large local, state, and municipal governance structures. While these served us well in times of rapid expansion and growth, they have outlived their usefulness.

If we applied the same standards of excellence developed in the private sector over the last 50 years to our local governments, we would see a magnitude of change. If a factory assembly line worker can have the power to "stop the production line," why couldn't Susie Q or Billy Bob citizen figure out the trash collection schedule? Yeah, I know someone is going to say "economies of scale." In today's hyper connected world, that argument no longer holds—but that's a topic for another blog/rant.

Co-production is coming alive in areas where the budget pressure is the greatest, specifically in Europe. We expect to see a similar trend in the US of A within two years. In closing, Co-Production is about working together for a strong community and social services that are more effective. It starts with the idea that services are successful only when the people served are involved. Teaching is an example. A teacher will teach, but learning happens when students engage. That principle can be taken into almost every field of service. If clients don't become actively engaged in achieving a successful outcome, the service provider will not succeed alone.

Community based government.

Frankly, a representative form of governance has become outmoded. Why couldn't citizens dial in to a council meeting and ask questions, even vote? Really, there is no longer a technical barrier—it is purely political. Want to reduce government overhead? Start by getting rid of 50% of elected officials and replace them with on-line discussion groups and webcasts. We have figured out how to do this in education and health care. Why not governance?

We have all witnessed the incredible power of social media this year. Political movements are learning to use the power of media very quickly—faster than the entrenched powers are learning. New tools pop up every day - like Google+. If history is any guide, we probably haven't seen the real community platform for decision making yet. However, things like http://ideascale.com/ are providing a glimpse of what can be.

The question is - which communities are going to move in this direction and be a guide for the rest of us? It will take a lot of will power to make the move. However, it is no longer a technical barrier. Let us have "working groups" that interact on-line most of the time, then have face-to-face "general assemblies" to reach consensus. OWS is showing us the way.

Another key to effective community based government is real time feedback. Right now, governance feedback could take two years—unless of course there is a recall election. One of the key principles of representative democracy was to have elected people stand in for their constituents and vote on behalf of their interests. Well somewhere between voter apathy and hyper financed campaigns the systems has broken down.

When it took two weeks to travel across the country, or a half-day from the farm to the City Hall that system made sense. It's no longer the case. We can still elect people to do "the people's business" but why not leverage technology to give these folks real time feedback and make the process transparent. You can make phone calls, send emails, and write blogs; but it is largely invisible to other constituents. Consider this, make all incoming and outgoing correspondence public and visible. Then we would know how many of our neighbors were (or were not) complaining about the same things. That might change the dynamic of the relationships between elected officials and the citizens who vote them into office.

The last point about community-based governance is the use (or non-use) of public facilities. There is a tremendous investment in infrastructure like courthouses, fire stations, office buildings, libraries and public works places; they we could re-purpose them and turn them over for civic use. Think about it, taxpayer investments are used perhaps 8 hours a day. What a waste of resources, but sharing them could be dangerous. If people knew where to go and it didn't cost anything, they just might, just might start to use these places to organize. Frightful thought.

This is the last barrier to community-based government. People need places to meet face-to-face and, dare I say, places to meet, plan and organize. Where better to meet than in those very symbols of public investment? Meet in the places that belong, ultimately, to the community.

When we look into our crystal ball, we see some evidence that all these things are starting to blossom. All it will take is a spark of innovation. The past decade of stagnant economic conditions and polarized politics has slowed the inevitable course of events. But it's coming. Just listen to the marketing pitch from an innovative residential village in the western US:

> "A place where Albuquerque's innovative spirit and respect for the environment, result in a healthier, simpler, and more sustainable way to live. A place where work and home and school and fun are within walking distance of each other. A place that will make a difference … for your business, your life and, at least in a small way, your world. Welcome to Mesa del Sol."

The Business End of a Sharp Stick[52]

We have talked about what it takes for a person and a community to thrive in the 21st Century. Last, but not least, we turn to the world of commerce and the six things you need to be aware of if you want YOUR business to thrive.

Know what your product lifecycle is

A product life cycle follows a technology adoption curve. The changing psychology of the marketplace has shifted many consumers from conservative late adopters to the more visionary early adopters. The critical challenge for many businesses, especially with the introduction of radically new and/or different products, is transitioning from the early market adoption to the mainstream market. The underlying psychology of these two groups is very different.

Integrate product with content and service

The old psychological belief system that "businesses are formed around products" has changed. It has shifted to the belief that "businesses are formed around service." People now expect more than just 'things.' They want to "be taught" how to use products properly and they want to know how using this product will improve their own work and quality of life.

Emphasize product marketing

Your business should be built around providing solutions <u>to your customer's business problems</u> and it should evolve ahead of their needs. Product marketing managers should act as 'producers' that take an idea from story line to finished movie and then move on to other projects.

Integrate horizontally with partners

Don't try to do everything. Integrate your business horizontally with strategic relationships. Remember to stay focused on your core competency and hire out everything else. This includes your internal administrative functions. Only do what you do best and find strategic relationships to do everything else.

Design real time, continuous customer feedback systems

Get into the hearts and minds of your customers - and STAY there. You need systems that are continuously monitoring your customers changes in beliefs and attitudes. This should be an internal function integrated into marketing.

Internet is only a compliment to other channels

Use e-commerce strategies as a compliment to existing sales and distribution channels. Emphasize content in the e-commerce channel. Use it primarily for customer education, information and feedback.

Fade to Black

So there you have it - how to not only survive, but also thrive in the 21st Century dominated by increasing uncertainty. We have outlined nine steps for you to follow, three things to make happen in your community, and six things to do to have a thriving business.

We hope you enjoyed the journey. This is a lot of information to digest. Take your time and be patient. You know how to find us if you want help. We're here to assist in the birth of this new social world.

> *When the student is ready, the teacher will appear.*
> *- Zen saying*

Epilogue – Some very specific predictions.

The fire serpent. Tibetan symbol for opening the chakras for attunement. It represents an opening to the future and an alignment of all energy levels toward purpose.

Epilogue – A Quick Look inside the Crystal Ball

No book portending to be about the future would be complete without a peek into the void beyond the present. So, here in our humble opinion are a few tantalizing thoughts about what we think is going to happen in the next few years.

Some Predictions About the Future of Work

This section is a re-print and update from an earlier document published by the Work Design Collaborative in 2005. Of the 28 predictions, we made then, 11 have come true by 2010. That's a 40% hit rate. Of the remainder, a number of them relate to structural changes in laws and regulations, which inherently lag significantly behind actual changes in social attitudes and behavior. We submit 17 of them for your consideration.

1. The human commercial activity we have called 'work' will cease to be the central activity of human existence in the developed world.

This will be especially true for conceptual based and creative tasks. As talent becomes scarcer, a premium will be placed on non-'work' activities. (80%, circa 2015) Look for terms like "work-life balance" to go away and terms like "Well-Being" and "Quality of life" to enter the vocabulary.

2. Centralized power and status structures will devolve.

Nation states, multinational corporations and institutionalized non-secular organizations will first lose status and trustworthiness among citizens, stakeholders and congregations. Corruption will weaken their trust bonds. Loss of power (defined as legalistic relations) will follow. In its place, localized communities will appear as loosely connected in federations on a planetary basis. (40%, circa 2013) Note: See Occupy Wall Street.

3. Work will be more collaborative, less individualistic

People will shift their work activities to their core competencies for approximately 80% of their time. Everything else will be handed off to someone with complimentary competencies. People will become less 'vertically integrated' and in favor of forming loosely coupled collaborative networks. No more, 'jack of all trades.' The remaining time will be devoted to learning new skills and competencies. (80%, 2013) There is an e of the "business of one," or more euphemistically "CEO of Me, Inc."

4. People (atoms) will combine into teams (molecules)

People will become highly networked for the duration of individual projects. Talent assembles into molecules of several people; stay together for a project, break apart and then form again into new molecular forms. Consider the working models in Hollywood where actors, directors and producers come together for a project only to disband and then re-group for another. (75%, 2015) The "Hollywood Model" becomes the norm.

5. Molecules will be short lived (half-life decreases from years to months)

As the Internet speeds up our social processes, projects take on new meanings and last only a brief time. The average project length will be one year, with a rarity of multiple year projects. The richness and variety of work available will motivate people toward a constant mix and re-mix of activities. Most knowledge workers will find themselves 'employed' on several projects simultaneously. (See above)

6. Back to guild structures

Guilds and 'confederations' will return as the primary social organizational model for smaller groups of people. Guilds will be responsible for recruitment of talent, training (more like mentoring) and enforcement of process quality standards. Guilds will be based on a common interest in a particular topic area or expertise, such as the Screen Actors Guild. (50%, 2015)

7. Corporations will morph into confederations with shared liability

Modern corporations are an artificial legal structure created within the past 100 years to minimize the risk associated with control of large asset bases. As Peter Drucker so aptly noted, they have out lived their usefulness. The assumptions, upon which they were formed, are no longer valid. A major organizing assumption was that large organizations were required to capitalize the investments required in the ownership of production, such as factories. With the shift from production to conceptual work, this assumption is no longer valid for most of our working population.

Instead, Confederations of business clusters will move to the forefront. They will be held together by strategy; not ownership of assets. (75%, 2013)

8. Work support structures will become a business in itself.

As the move towards individualism (i.e., free agency) approaches 20% of the workforce, the need for different workforce support structures will emerge as a business opportunity in itself. Agencies (aka the old term was "Companies") that provide marketing and administrative services, retirement plan memberships, and group health insurance to this group of workers will grow in numbers and flourish. (90%, 2014)

9. Employment law will change to recognize a new category of relationship; that of people to organization

In the early years of the 21st century two basic forms of worker/company relationships existed in the United States and most other industrialized countries. There was either an employee/employer relationship or a contractor relationship. Both of these forms proved to be inadequate for the new, more agile and fluid kinds of social relationships required by knowledge workers (the creative class). Limited Liability Corporations or Partnerships pioneered in the legal, accounting and consulting professions are the nascent forms of these new relationships. Individuals will become in essence a 'company of one' and band together for projects—that may be short lived formal organizations for limited periods. (90%, 2013) New employment laws will be a pre-requisite and this will hinge on the political landscape in the US and solidarity of the EU.

10. Compensation will be based on customer effectiveness

As we move from a commodity production base (in the First world) to a service and knowledge economy; creative talent will be compensated based on how the outcomes. For example, Doctors are compensated for keeping people well; professors are compensated based on incomes of former students; accountants on wealth created; executives on five plus years return on investor's money. The question will be "what did I do to make your life easier, longer, more satisfying?" not "how long did it take me to do it?" (60%, 2015)

11. The basic metaphor of business will change from battalion maneuvers to special operations

The work world of the future will look more like an Olympic basketball game than a baseball game. Constantly shifting roles, responsibilities and competencies for success will be the hallmark. Brute force will be replaced by stealth process. This implies the demise of the logic of 'economies of scale,' which characterized the industrial age. Bigger isn't better; and nimble becomes a good thing. Social interaction in the workplace will move from highly scripted, stable interactions such as those found in the cathedral to the spontaneous, often raucous, patterns of the village meetinghouse. (90%, 2015)

12. Frontier mentality as opposed to city dweller

People will adopt a more singular, 'I'm responsible for myself' attitude in their work relations. America will 'de-cluster the workforce' and de-massify large urban areas, except for the new immigrants, marginalized sub-groups and young unattached populations. Individualized action will be valued more than close neighborly patterns of highly dense locales. (90%, 2014)

13. Context of relationship changes from livelihood to life-quality enhancing

The social context of the relationship, between workers and 'employers,' will shift from a earning a livelihood to life quality enhancing for the individual. This force will cause the redefinition of the implied social contract between people and companies, the source of their livelihood. (70%, 2014)

14. Company brand attracts talent

People will be attracted to companies largely based on their brand. Not having a strong brand identity will neutralize attempts to attract and retain talent. A negative brand perception will actually repel talent. Branding factors such as interesting, varied work are positive. As are existence of other 'cool' people and challenges toward growth. (90%, 2013)

15. A new grammar will emerge to define and describe human commercial activity.

The English language (as well as others) evolves continuously. The advent of the Internet as an international medium of common communication has given rise to things like blogs (on-going conversations) and wiki's (communal dictionaries). These mediums are the message. Look here for the new language. (60%, 2015)

16. The conceptual dots will be disconnected

The artificial connections between people, organizations and society will decompose and a new higher order will emerge. An emerging realization of the interconnectedness of 'everything' will presage an almost mystical realization that human civilization is rapidly evolving to a new order. Revolutionary advances in technology (e.g., robotics and bio-tech) will finally directly impact human development and longevity. (70%, 2015)

17. The social texture of companies will change

Instead of having implicit rules of behavior and action coming from commonly accepted social values, business molecules will generate their own rationality. The texture of a work organization will come from its connectedness in action. Hierarchies flatten; relationships are based more on respect and "status given" not power. Just like a crossword puzzle, the work unit will take on more meaning 'as it is filled in' by action. (80%, 2013).

Ricochet Shots: Game Changers

Of course, as uncertainty increases (one of our mega trends), unpredictable things can happen. As we peer into the crystal ball, there are some things, which could be game changers in the next 5 years. Don't ask how we come up with these things, it is totally an intuitive process. And before you nattering nabobs of negativity begin chattering, we deliberately like to think the unthinkable and challenge the existing state of knowledge.

Here's our stab at it. We sort these over the edge predictions into four categories that are really the bedrock of the global social economy. If we were wagering people these are four areas, we'd invest everything we could get our hands on.

Water: Water is rapidly becoming THE critical resource for the sustainability of the human race. We believe that some fundamental discoveries in organic chemistry will yield a low cost, low technology process to create fresh water supplies from renewable natural resources. After all, it's just oxygen and hydrogen, right.

Energy: This one is close. Check out Bloom Energy and the most recent advances in solar film technology. We believe that some basic discoveries in particle physics will upset the typical discovery, extraction, refining, transportation and storage energy paradigm. It will be like when fire became portable and could be turned on and off. One could argue that this event alone would transform almost overnight the current geopolitical map of the planet.

Manufacturing: Currently 3D printing is all the rage. As this technology, advances we think that developments in the material sciences will yield substances that can be phase changing; for example objects could be printed in malleable form and then transformed into hardened materials. Localized manufacturing of "hard goods" at a fraction of today's cost. Think of the implications for the global labor markets.

Organizations/Institutions: OK, we saved our favorite for the last. You have seen hints and glimpses of this one throughout the book. Most human institutions today are basically modeled on physical forms. Hard, permanent, in dominion over nature. The best example is Egyptian pyramids and bureaucrats. OK, it's a stretch but think about it. The coming forms are going to be more like fractals where every part mirrors every other part. The dynamics will follow toriordal patterns. Constant flow of energy in orthogonal vectors while rotating. Take a close look at the energy flows in a galaxy.

Now we are drifting off into the realm of metaphysics, quantum theory and vibratory energy fields. We'll stop here and re-visit these later. However, if any of you care to talk to us about these things, we are open.

Notice we did not say much about "hard" technology, medical science, and robotics or space exploration. We have thoughts but are out of time. We'll close with a quote from the Great Gretkzy:

"I skate to where the puck is going to be, not where it is."

Solving the Puzzle

Closing the space now.........

We started out with a teaser. We said there was a larger, overall plan to this book, and challenged you to figure it out. The time has come to reveal the secret.

The pattern is the human body chakras. Starting with the "Backstory" as the Ground chakra and running upwards to the "Doing, Being and Living" chapter representing the Crown chakra. Then we added some mind/body stretching. The "Thriving" chapter is the "transpersonal point" where we humans connect with the high planes of vibration energy. And the Epilogue is intended to be the point where we reach across space and time into the future. So there it is. Hope you enjoyed it.

Now let's go back at look at the plan of the book from Chapter 0.

Chapter	Question Answered	Theme	Chakra[1]	Energy Realized
0-Backstory	Where did this come from?	Conception and birth of the idea	Earth or Ground	Shaping in-flowing energy
1-Drivers of change	What is manifesting?	Potentiality	Root	Physical
2-Purpose	What is your purpose?	Giving and Receiving	Sacral	Emotional
3- New Skills	What will be required?	Karma "cause and effect"	Solar Plexus	Ego
4- Artisans of Thought	What does it look like?	Minimal Effort	Heart	Social
5-New Workplace	How is it done?	Intention	Throat	Creativity
6-New Community	How is it perceived or seen?	Detachment	Third Eye	Intuition
7-Doing, Being and Living	How is it to be understood?	Dharma "Purpose in life"	Crown	Understanding
8-Thriving	What is the conscious connection?	Expanding beyond current limits	Transpersonal Point	Transformation
9-Epilogue	What if ………?	A look into the futurescope		The unbroken circle
Resources	How to find a teacher?	Moving to the next level		Completing the pattern

---

[1] Themes are derived from "The Seven Spiritual Laws of Success" Deepak Chopra (1994) New World: San Rafael, CA.

[2] The chakras are based on the "Hara Line" from the study of Reiki. An extension of the traditional seven-body chakra's, Diane Stein, "Essential Reiki" (1995) The Crossings Press, Berkeley, CA

Resources

We have grouped suggested resources by chapter and added them on, here, at the end of our e-book. The idea is not to detract from readability of the main message and allow readers quick, easy access to more information by topic area. A bit unorthodox but this whole project is like that.

The resources vary by chapter. In some cases we offer up assessment tools, in other cases more typical bibliographic information. Each chapter is different because each topic is different.

One more thought. This is an extremely dynamic environment. We did not even attempt to offer up a complete and comprehensive set of resources—it changes every day. We invite you to visit our website (FutureWorkingTogether.com) for current updates. And if you really want to get down in the weeds on any of these topics—just contact us.

The Meanings of the Symbols

We're sure you have noticed that we like to use symbols. There are a couple of reasons for that. First, we are becoming an increasing symbolic world and we need to learn how to think symbolically. An art our ancestors were masterful at, but something we seem to have lost with becoming "civilized". Second, symbols connect us with a higher state of consciousness if you will.

The symbols we use come from two primary sources; Ancient Native American Indian religions and more contemporary Eastern traditions. It really reflects Charliepedia's Native heritage (25% Cherokee) and his recent study and practice of Rekei Master/Teacher.

Symbol for a blending if triple realms. Blending of the three authors thoughts. Technically called a "triskele". Ancient Celtic in origin. Sometimes seen as the trinity. For us a bringing together of will, being and function.

 Symbol for change. African Adinkra symbol MMERE DANE originated from the Akan people in Ghana and represents the changes and dynamics of life. Many things occur beyond our direct control (or the illusion of control) this symbol reminds us to not resist these forces but blend with them.

 Purpose. Reiki symbol Cho Ku Rei meaning "place the power of the universe here". The power is within you, it only needs to be recognized and activated.

 Leadership. Symbolizes three levels of existence and the need for leaders to bring these levels together. Many places of origin among Norse tribes and West African religions.

 The dragonfly from Hopi traditions. There is a double meaning here. It represents an ability to get past self-imposed limits and achieve new goals. On the other hand, the dragonfly represents quickness, agility and invincibility.

 The hand represents presence of man, his work and achievements. Recognizes man as a vessel for creative power. In our interpretation it is the PLACE where this creative activity takes place.

 Eye of the medicine man. A symbol of wisdom and awareness. Where does it come from—in our view it comes from the learning community, the new guild. This is where the medicine man lives.

 The medicine wheel, or circle of life. A physical manifestation of spiritual energy. A bringing together of all the pieces needed to give breathe to life and sustain it.

The enneagram. We take it from the tradition of Sufi mysticism brought to us in the works of G. I. Gurdjeiff and J.G. Bennett. It represents a process of continuous coming into being and improvement from one cycle to the next.

The fire serpent. Tibetan symbol for opening the chakras for attunement. It represents an opening to the future and an alignment of all energy levels toward purpose.

Chapter 0 Resources

So where is your company in relationship to these dimensions? Here's simple, quick and easy way to find out. Answer the questions, score them yourself and then lay them out on a simple grid like Figure 0-1. If you'd like to know more, please contact us for a complimentary detailed analysis.

To assess your organizations' level of interaction, answer the following scoring 1 for low; 2 for medium and 3 for high. Then total your scores.

		Low	Medium	High
1	People here try to make friends and to keep their relationships strong			
2	People here get along very well			
3	People in our group often socialize outside the office			
4	People here really like one another			
5	When people leave our group, we stay in touch			
6	People here do favors for others because they like one another			
7	People here often confide in one another about personal matters			

To assess your organization's level of freedom, answer the following in the same manner.

1. Our group (organization, division, unit, team) understands and shares the same business objectives

2. Work gets one effectively and productively

3. Our group takes strong action to address poor performance

4. Our collective will to win is high

5. When opportunities for competitive advantage arise, we move quickly to capitalize on them

6. We share the same strategic goals

7. We know who the competition is

Resources

"Current Workplace Trends" lecture delivered by Frank Duffy to the Sun/BPAmoco Blue Chalk II Design session, Oct 30-Nov 1, 1999, Palo Alto, CA.

What Holds the Modern Company together?, Rob Goffee and Gareth Jones, Harvard Business Review, Nov-Dec 1996, pp. 133-148.

"Organigraphics: Drawing How companies Really Work:, H. Mintzberg and L. Vander Hayden. Harvard Business Review, Sep-Oct 1999, pp. 87-94.

The Age of Social Transformation by Peter Drucker , Appearing in the Atlantic Monthly, November 1994. A survey of the epoch that began early in this century, and an analysis of its latest manifestations: an economic order in which knowledge, not labor or raw material or capital, is the key resource; a social order in which inequality based on knowledge is a major challenge; and a polity in which government cannot be looked to for solving social and economic problems. 20 pages.

The Future at Work — Trends and Implications Lynn A. Karoly and Constantijn W.A. Panis, *The 21st Century at Work: Forces Shaping the Future Workforce and Workplace in the United States*, MG-164-DOL, 2004

Trends in workforce size and composition and in the pace of technological change and economic globalization will have implications for the future of work. Employees will work in more decentralized, specialized firms; slower labor growth will encourage employers to recruit groups with relatively low labor force participation; greater emphasis will be placed on retraining and lifelong learning; and future productivity growth will support higher wages and may affect the wage distribution. Given this, some policies may need to be reexamined.

Diagnosing Organizational Culture

http://haworth.com/Brix?pageID=241

Defining Culture and Organizational Culture: From Anthropology to the Office

http://haworth.com/Brix?pageID=241

Organizational Culture Annotated Bibliography

http://haworth.com/Brix?pageID=241

The resources for this chapter are meant more to guide conversations than to offer confirming evidence. Some references are included as endnotes in the chapter.

Chapter 1 Resources

Emergent Vocabulary

These are words that we see coming up more and more. Look them up and start using them to describe your own experience

Co-production	Leapfrog	Greenfield
Psychonaut	Inspiration beyond belief	Massive systems dysfunction
Economic gardening	Economic gardening	Pain is a re-set button
Ignorance over time is extinction	Exponomy	New~grammar
Uncertainty~risk	Coworking	Surface~versus~substance
Words~duality	Work~unity	Wordless~oneness
Contagion	Re-birthing	Authentic~community
Self-Actualization	Purpose	Consciousness
Presence	Accountability	Systems
Beyond~Duality		

Vision

How to get there

- Individuals
- Companies
- Communities

Ground (ask these questions to find out what grounds people)

1. Do you have faith in your own potential?
2. Is human nature basically good or bad?
3. Does true knowledge come from external or internal sources?

A political conservative in our Western culture would answer:

> 1. Little to none. I am at the mercy of uncontrollable forces.
>
> 2. Basically bad. Needs to be controlled. (A corollary here is that these types think they are the terrible people and display lots of outward directly hostility and anger)
>
> 3. True knowledge is given to us by outside authorities and should not be questioned.

Tools

How do you see people?

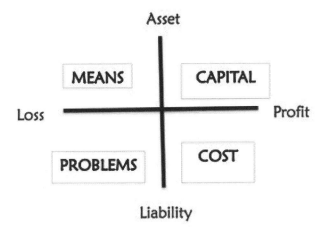

Direction

1. Who are you?
2. What is your passion?
3. What is your intention?

Workplace Strategy Formation Process

Community Design Institute Discovery Workshop

The challenge every business faces is how to build and provision a future oriented, agile workplace that attracts and retains key talent.

The way in which economic value is produced has changed. In fact, the very nature of work itself has changed dramatically over the last several years. Talent has replaced raw materials and financial resources as the core driver of economic value.

Furthermore, work, and the wealth associated with it, now flows to where the talent resides. And the talent pool that drives wealth includes both young and mature workers, all of who are seeking high quality-of-life areas to live and work in.

Strategic business development must now be focused on attracting creative talent to your enterprise. The key to building a sustainable enterprise involves enabling state-of-the-art workplaces where participants work on projects, collaborate on ideas, and share resources. This strategy not only increases the quality of life of employees but also helps to create hundreds, if not thousands, of new jobs in the local economies.

The key questions have become:

- ❖ What is *your* business doing to adapt to the new economic model?

- ❖ What should you be doing to become a place where creative talent wants to live and work?

- ❖ What are you doing to leverage the new technologies that stitch together work, education, and community life?

We have developed a one-day Discovery Workshop[sm] to help businesses journey towards the future by leveraging their core competencies and linking their economy into the emerging global workplace.

The Discovery Workshop[sm]

We work with leaders to convene a one-day workshop designed to accomplish four goals:

- ❖ Clarify trends in the global economy and identify the fundamental drivers of change;
- ❖ Explore the implications of these changes for your business;
- ❖ Identify opportunities for leveraging or supplementing your business assets;
- ❖ Agree on next steps for moving ahead

Our Method: Visioning Process Design

Our principals are highly skilled at facilitating this group discovery process. Clarity of vision and agreement on methods is a foundation for action.

The diamond figure depicted below is a graphic depiction of a four-phase process we use to help local leaders articulate their vision. The process of using this thinking tool involves moving around the diamond from ISSUE IDENTIFICATION to DIRECTION, to VISION, and finally to METHODS.

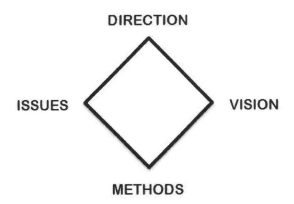

Thinking About Visioning

ISSUE IDENTIFICATION: The basis for engaging in this process. Here we go back and clearly outline where the business core strategy is coming from and why. In this discovery process you will examine: (1) the values articulated by leaders and (2) the trends in business development from a local, regional, and national perspective. The Community Design Institute will provide data drawn from its research to provide a basis for this discussion and answer to your question.

DIRECTION: What is the general direction of your business sector's future? We help you look closely at the maximum potential you have for steering your own course. We explore opportunities for forging alliances with other's to build critical mass and collaborative support capabilities. The question here is, what is the core competency of your business? How do you build on that competency to create new opportunities and new strengths?

VISION: Your core vision is a clear, consensual expression of what will your company look like when your goals have been realized. We help you develop a preliminary vision statement in terms that can be tested in the future.

METHOD(S): This is the last step in the Discovery Workshop. It involves charting a path forward with specific action steps. There are three questions that must be addressed:

1. What resources are needed to make the vision a reality?

2. What do we have in place today?

3. Where do we go for the rest?

At the conclusion of the Discovery Workshop you will have answers to the following critical questions:

- ❖ What are the key characteristics of local labor demand for the next five to ten years (i.e., skills, needs, competencies)?

- ❖ What infrastructure will be required to support a revitalized (but highly distributed) workforce (i.e., technology, physical plant, transportation, local support services)?

- ❖ What public policy programs will be required to support the workforce of the future in your community?

- ❖ What are other local communities (sources of talent) already doing to develop themselves into "talent magnets?"

- ❖ What are the specific issues that need to be addressed as you define the steps for action?

- ❖ What are the specific actions steps you need to take to move forward?

Chapter 2 Resources

There are two major resources for here for you to help in defining your purpose. Of course, there is vast amount of literature on this topic, but we are very practical and want to give you something you can start using right now. First, let's begin with how to select your own personal Board of Directors. Lastly, a description of what the career lattice practice, the individual's starting point for Adapt! Advantage is about. If you are intrigued, reach out to us.

The Personal Board of Directors—Charliepedia's version

Who – criteria

I think all of us need our own Personal Board of Directors, a place where we can go and seek council and get advice or new knowledge to help guide us in our own transitions. So, you may ask yourself, "What's the difference between this and just my friends"? Well, the basic difference is that this is a small group of people, usually 5 to 7 that you have deliberately sought out and brought together to help guide you in periods and times of transition. It's not necessarily based on family, physical community, the workplace or historical accident.

So, what are the criteria for selecting members of your own personal Board of Directors? I think you need to look at the factors that can help you realize you were full potential. Finding people who have some expertise in those areas, who are compatible with you from a personality perspective and finally those who can offer you some critical balance in the areas that are to your strong suit. So for example, if you're a person who pays attention to the world in a broad- external fashion as we saw on the TAIS, seek out someone in your Board of Directors who has as their natural focus a narrow- internal perspective. This will help balance you're decisions.

I think you need someone who can advise you on personal decisions, crisis of consciousness and ethical matters. You also need someone who is very sensitive to the larger issues of the business community and personal finance. Third, you need someone who can help you continuously improve, such as an educational adviser or someone who specializes in transitions. Then I think you need an older, wiser person. A mentor. Someone who's been there, done that and can keep you from making mistakes along your pathway. I think there needs to be another person on your Board of Directors who really is what I called "the Challenger". You need to have one very strong person, who ultimately has your best interests at heart, but will always challenge you on any anticipated decision and won't simply go along with you. Your ideal Personal Board of Directors

- **Ethical advisor**
- **Financial matters**
- **Education**
- **Mentor**
- **Challenger**

How to Select

So, this looks like about five people playing all these different roles. That's whom you need. But how do you go about finding these folks? Sit down and go through your address book with a list of these roles and start to put names next to them. By doing this, you'll develop a list of candidates. The next step is to interview them. Sit down with each of these people and explain to them what your transition processes is like and what you're doing. In short, recruit them; explain to them what role you would like them to play and what you expect from them. As strange as this may sound, it is not difficult to do.

My own experience has been that you will find people very receptive to this idea, quite thrilled by the concept and actually honored that you asked them to play this new role in your life. You may find yourself actually entering into a reciprocal relationship with some of your Board of Directors. You may be able to perform a like role for them.

Selection of the final group of people on your Board should be done, only after you shared with them the results of your own assessment, clarified your own direction of change and getting them to agree to play the role. Finally, I think it comes down to your own courage about how strong you want this group of advisers to be. This will be the group that perhaps tells you not to enter into a business venture, break off a relationship or other significant event you don't like to confront.

You are placing yourself in a position to deliberately seek external feedback and guidance -- that sometimes you won't want to hear what they have to say. So, select them carefully, and make sure that you are putting together a group that offers you considerable diversity and approach and opinions. And that they at the end of the day are motivated to help you improve and continuously be, effective in a new world of work.

Frequency of interaction

How frequently should you seek them out and ask questions and review with them actions that you are contemplating. I think they are needed on a regular basis as you would with any other counselor. How often do you see your accountant? How often do you set down with your attorney? Or perhaps, how often do you seek the council of a minister, pastor or other spiritual leader? You have your own rhythm to your decision-making process and you should use your Board of Directors at the same pace and time frame.

I seek out my own Personal Board of Directors usually on a quarterly basis or more frequently if there are significant events such as opportunities for major new projects. Also, on an annual basis for a review of my own personal development plan and my business plan with my Board looking for places that need to be adjusted or changed. And of course, they are available for individual conversations should matters pop-up.

Removal and Upgrade

What about removal? You can certainly fire any of your members at your discretion. I think that you should review your needs and how your board has been meeting them every couple of years or so. In the dynamic business environment we're in, you may need to change out individual Board members to bring in different perspectives and backgrounds ahead of the times that you need to make decisions in these areas. Always be on the look out for people who can offer you advice for development in ways you can't even anticipate today. You're Board of Directors should be a dynamic guidance system and one that you can modify to the your needs over time.

The Sevenfold Work "The Path Forward"[53]

We started this chapter by talking about the necessity to make personal transitions and realize your true purpose. Now we are at a point in our journey where we need to look at just how we're supposed to be able to make this transition. Considering that we have a fairly good understanding of who we are, how we interact with others, and how we take in information; we're now at the point to decide what's the process that can move us forward and become more comfortable and be effective in the new world of work. So let's begin. There's a seven-step process that you can use to guide yourself through this transition. Please note that this "sevenfold" pattern is also the basis to the leadership development process detailed in Chapter 3.

The table below outlines these steps in the order you'll take them. For each step you'll see the name of the *state* associated with that step, the *quality* you should be feeling during that particular stage of transition and the *activity* you'll associate with that step.

Table 2-3: Sevenfold Work

Step	State	Quality	Activity
1	Initiation	Assimilation: Active taking from outside to inside. Your focus is on your WORLD	Awareness that something is lacking and time is passing. You move to get something you need. You begin seeking answers to 'nagging' questions; "Why am I so anxious all the time?"

2	Involvement	<u>Struggle:</u> Active inside ourselves to inside ourselves. Your focus is on MYSELF	Looking at the internal states we don't want to look at. Introspection. "Is it me or is everyone around here nuts?"
3	Separation	<u>Service:</u> Active from inside to outside. Your focus is on COMMUNITY	Duty, intentional suffering. Sharing what we know to build future capability in others. Giving of oneself to others, usually seen as 'community service' actions. It gives us emotional room to separate from old patterns and to focus on something outside ourselves.
4	Harmonization	<u>Manifestation</u>	Tao. We are a vehicle through which creativity is expressed. The 'flow state'. You begin to act in new ways, building off the old and feel re-juventated.

5	Insight	<u>Receptivity:</u> Opening up to take in from the outside. Your focus is on COMMUNITY	Being open to help from others. Trust the universe to bring you what you need. Relaxation and openness knowing that you are firmly committed to a pathway of change.
6	Renunciation	<u>Submission:</u> Receptive inside to inside. Your focus is on MYSELF	Letting go of ego. Emptying the vessel within of baggage. Moving from 'selfishness' to improving your state of being.
7	Completion	<u>Purity:</u> Receptive to what is beyond us. Your focus is on your WORLD	Waking up!! Consciousness comes to us. Realization of your part in the universe, a spiritual awakening.

Adapt! Career Latticing Series

Avadon is committed to helping professionals and students alike develop their career paths. To address the knowledge areas listed above and additionally the top soft skills demanded by business today, The Avadon Group series, Career Latticing Services (CLS), helps participants better understand what it takes to compete in today's marketplace and well as in the future. The Avadon Group's series takes this understanding further by focusing on the following outcomes:

Better understanding of what it takes to compete—
 In a rapidly changing, global marketplace;

Increased productivity and output—
 By connecting the dots between personal impact to fluid expectations and objectives of employers.

Greater alignment—
 Between employer and individual brands, values and goals.

Increased sense of control—
 By focusing on actions individuals control and establishing that it's a *personal choice* to enhance career opportunities, and potentially, quality of life.

Greater adaptability--
 By understanding requirements of a rapidly changing marketplace of people to quickly flex personal competencies.

...all of which helps participants seize opportunities and bounce back from unforeseen changes. You not only understand opportunities but have a plan to capitalize on market trends and to respond to changing workplace conditions with flexibility and *agility*. The CLS series workbooks for transition are available for download at: http://www.avadongroup.com/html/courses.html or email fwt@futureworkingtogether.com.

Chapter 3 Resources

Resources for this chapter are a bit more traditional in format. Endnotes in the chapter point you in the right direction. The majority of this material has been published in the peer reviewed literature.

Development Programs

Contact us for a program flyer

Technical References

Cameron, Kim (2008) Positive *Leadership*, San Francisco: Berrett Koehler.

Chopra, Deepak (2010) *The Soul of Leadership*, New York: Harmony.

Daft, R.L. and Lengel, R.H. (2000), Fusion Leadership, San Francisco: Berrett-Koehler.

Forrester, Jay (1963) *Industrial Dynamics*, Cambridge, Massachusetts: MIT Press.

Garvin, David (2000) *Learning in Action*, Boston: Harvard Business School Press.

Grantham, C., Ware, J., and Williamson, C., (2007) *Corporate Agility*, New York: AMACOM.

Grantham, C. (2011) **"Leadership for the 21st Century:, in *Work on the Move*, Arnold et al, IFMA Foundation, Houston, Texas.**

Kuchinsky, Saul (1987) *Systematics*, West Virginia: Claymont Communications.

Pink, Dan (2006), A Whole New Mind New York: Riverhead Trade (Penguin Group).

Roach, Geshe Michael (2000), *The Diamond Cutter: The Buddha on Strategies for Managing Your Business and Your Life*, New York, Doubleday.

Senge, Peter (2006) *The Fifth Discipline*, New York: Broadway Business (Crown Publishing).

Web Sources

http://en.wikipedia.org/wiki/Leadership_development

http://www.comm-design.net

Chapter 4 Resources

Artisans of Thought Resources

There are numerous endnotes with links to web resources in the chapter itself. Here we would like to present two additional resources. First, an example of new kind of "artisan" resume and then a brief guide on how to craft a positioning statement for your inner artisan.

Resume

Sample Positioning Description for an Artisan of Thought

- Position description or Project Deliverables
- Resume of hiring manager or client
- Statement of conditions of success

Who Am I

A producer. Strengths are Connectedness, Strategic, Ideation, Woo and Maximizer

Flat spot: Administrivia, busy work.

What do I do best?

Create integrated content that informs strategic business decisions.

Example: SCAN. How to leverage FoW workplace into picking new markets by matching labor pool with customer needs.

Track Record

- Two institutes, one corporate R&D Division over 20+ years
- 7 Books, 20+ technical articles
- 800 citations
- FoW Brand ID (you found me)

What can I do for you?

- Build brand recognition
- Thought leadership
- Add value beyond product and service
- Help clients understand how to leverage your business to better service their customers
- (Strategic Customer Service)

Expectations

- Compensation at 75% of peer group
- Autonomy of operation
- Connection to resources I need
- Use what I produce
- Recognition

Crafting a statement

Craft what you want to say to take charge of the frame. You may work with either format

Framing Format *	"**I believe in** ..." followed by two strong progressive value words for a total of 27 words to be delivered in 9 seconds
1-Minute Statement:	"**I believe in** ..." followed by two strong progressive value words followed by about 200 words to be delivered in about 1 minute.

Each One-Minute Statement will begin with, "**I believe in** ..." followed by two strong progressive value words. Lakoffs "Ten-Word Philosophy for Progressives" contained in ***Don't Think of An Elephant*** are a good list. There are others.

Some helpful values to incorporate:

A Ten-Word Philosophy for Progressives

Stronger America	Stronger on defense, the economy, education; more effective in the world
Broad prosperity	Markets that provide every American a fair opportunity to prosper
Better future	Investing in improvement of the economy, education and the environment
Effective government	Clean, honest, efficient, and

155

	effective government working for a better future
Mutual responsibility	Values of families and communities: caring and responsibility

Another Useful List

Fairness	Fairness is unbiased distribution
Responsibility	Progressive responsibility is connected with the surface frame [concept] of fulfilling a need through empathy and using the common wealth for the common good. An illustrative example of this is Hurricane Katrina.
Freedom	Uncontested freedom is (very roughly) defined as being able to do what you want to do, providing you don't interfere with the freedom of others. This includes physical freedom, freedom to pursue goals, freedom of the will, and political freedom, where citizens freely choose who runs the state and where the state, by law, cannot interfere with the basic freedoms of its citizens
Equality	Equality of outcome is therefore not identical outcomes but the same

range of outcomes regardless of race. So, we would expect that given equality of opportunity (as there should be in |

	a democracy, and in a fair capitalist system), there would be equality of distribution of outcome.
Integrity	The basic logic of integrity is twofold. First, it means saying what you believe and then acting on it consistently. Second, it means the consistent application of a principle: Progressive integrity is the consistent application of nurturance.
Security	The uncontested core of security is providing protection through strength.[Progressive version is security through protection, not the knee jerk use of force.]

The last part of your framing work is to anticipate their talking points and have properly framed responses. That is a separate worksheet. A properly framed response uses the values and key words you developed above, but applies them in responding to their talking point. Remember, if you don't get the frame right, they won't hear your facts, no matter how good they are.

Resources—Chapter 5

Additional resources for this chapter on Business Community Centers^sm are proprietary. Full disclosure here is that the FwT tribe is engaged with a number of groups around the US in bringing this idea to market.

We have developed an extensive set of tools, techniques and benchmark data around a set of topics:

- Locational analysis—how to locate these centers. Region, city, neighborhood

- Design process—what is the form and function of the interior from a social technical perspective.

- Value added—service menu and description for end customer value add

- Brand—what it is and how to form it

- Corporate positioning—marketing package for corporate business center members

- Business model—Generic business plan for one center and also a national network of centers. All the due diligence, competitive analysis and financial models are included.

Please contact us for additional information.

Allocation of Energy
"A framework for action"

Stop doing ⬇	Slow down ↘	Maintain ➡	Speed up ↗	Start ⬆

Allocation of Energy *Instructions*

As you go through the next 2 days, we want you to note specific actions in your everyday life that fit into this allocation of energy framework. What is it that you need to stop, slow down, maintain, speed up and start that will help you turn the ideas presented here into reality?

The energy you free up from stopping or slowing something down gives you the resources to speed up and start new things. These items can be projects, relationships, or information resources.

Chapter 6 Resources

Back to a traditional format in terms of resources. This idea is fairly well developed and available in the open literature. The "how do you do it" is the subject of the next chapter.

References and Resources

Braudel, Fernand: (1982) *The Wheels of Commerce*, vol. II of *Civilization and Capitalism*, Harper and Row, New York.

Bressler, Stacy. and Grantham, Charles. (2000), *Communities of Commerce,* McGraw-Hill, New York.

Epstein, S. R. and Prak, Mararten, eds. (2008)*Guilds, Innovation, and the European Economy, 1400–1800.* Cambridge University Press, New York.

Grafe, Regina, and Oscar Gelderblom. (2010), "The Rise and Fall of the Merchant Guilds: Re-thinking the Comparative Study of Commercial Institutions in Premodern Europe," *Journal of Interdisciplinary History*, Spring, Vol. 40 Issue 4, pp 477–511.

Grantham, Charles. (2005) *The Future of Work*, McGraw-Hill, New York

Grantham, Charles and Semenchuk, J. (2003), "Gutenberg Wired: How the Printing Press Changed Everything and How the Internet is Doing it Again", White Paper, Community Design Institute (www.comm-design.net)

Grantham, Charles. (2000) Hollywood: A Business Model for the Future" Proceedings of the ACM SIG on Computer Personnel Research, Chicago, IL, pp. 47-60.

Grantham, Charles. (2012)"The Rebirth of Guilds" in Prethinking Work, Jeschke, S., Hees, F., Richert, A and Trantow, S. (eds.) LIT-Verlag, Frankfurt, Germany.

Malone, Thomas. and Rockart, J. (1991), "Computers, Networks and the Corporation" - Scientific American Special Issue on Communications, Computers, and Networks, September.

Prak, Maarten A.O. (ed.)(2006), *Craft Guilds in the Early Modern Low Countries: Work, Power and Representation.* Ashgate, The Netherlands.

Ogilvie, Sheilagh (2004) "Guilds, efficiency, and social capital: evidence from German proto-industry," *Economic History Review,* May Vol. 57 Issue 2, pp 286-333.

Ogilvie, Sheilagh, "Rehabilitating the Guilds: A Reply," *Economic History Review* vol 61 (2008), 175–182

Rouche, Michel, (1987) "Private life conquers state and society," in *A History of Private Life* vol I, Paul Veyne, editor, Harvard University Press, Boston.

Weyrauch, Thomas. (1999)Craftsmen and their Associations in Asia, Africa and Europe (Wettenberg/Germany, VVB Laufersweiler.

Chapter 7 Resources

Talent Integration Ecosystem^{SM} – Overall Plan

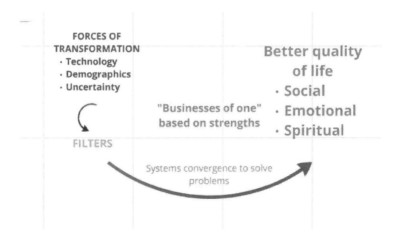

Talent Integration Ecosystem[sm] Framework—Getting Started

Instructions

In our view, there are three interdependent levels of activity to create a talent integration ecosystem. You may think of the process of developing innovative talent as a pipeline that has three stages of pumps, which add more energy, and speeds up the flow of talent.

We want you to walk away with an action plan for you, your community and your commercial activity. The first step is to deeply analyze what the true potential is in your world. The matrix on the next page is a thinking tool to help you do just that.

For each of the columns (citizen {that's you}; community and commerce) there are five questions, which need to be answered. Answer each in short from—two to ten words only. Do this quickly and don't try to over analyze the situation.

Once you have this work picture complete, you can move to action planning. Your final task is to take these answers and turn them into specific, concrete and doable actions. The last page is a template for your action plan, a playbook for continual guidance. Fill it out with one item for each of the 15 cells in the action framework table. Don't worry you can go back and modify as your particular situation demands. Great news! You have a checklist and a detailed plan now.

One option some people choose is to share this with a colleague, a friend or mentor. Then you can re-visit it every once in awhile as a progress checklist.

Talent Integration Ecosystem^{sm} - Action Framework

	Citizen	**Community**	**Commerce**
What do we need to be paying attention to?	*Leadership capabilities*	*Current system of dysfunctional governance*	*Development of ways to measure value added by thoughts and innovation*
What are we capable of doing with current resources?	*Creating small action groups*	*Muddling through with no systemic change*	*Random, un-coordinated activities*
What is our maximum potential?	*Assume formal elected positions*	*Developing community based sustainable governance*	*Collaborative, conscious systems of creativity and evolution*
What can we anticipate will oppose us in this transformation?	*Our own resistance to change*	*Existing political power structures and money*	*Old industrial order and laws of commercial activity*
What is the force energizing us? Or What is becoming necessary?	*The need for self-actualization*	*Demand for sustainability in our world*	*Global interconnectedness*

Action Plan

1. Do a self-assessment of my own capabilities

2.

3. Organize a "meet up" kind of gathering to discuss sustainable communities

4.

5......8.

9.

10. Do an inventory of local entrepreneurs using the SBDC or co-working facility

11.

Books to Read

Consumer Evolution (2007) Grantham, C. and Carr, J., John Wiley, NY

The Coming Jobs War (2011) Clifton, J., Gallup Press, NY

When the Boomers Bail (2011) Lautman, M., Logan Square, Albuquerque, NM

Chapter 8 Resources—Thriving

Most of these additional resources relate to the 9E® process. Although the process is pretty much self contained we included here as a necessary, but not sufficient, first step in thriving.

3 Page Action Plan for a thriving community

1. What is the problem?

   a. What are you proposing to do that will make people's lives better or easier?

2. What's the overall strategy for solving this problem?

3. What tactics will you need to use?

4. Logistics and support

   a. Include time/cost rough estimates

5. What alliances/partnerships will you need?

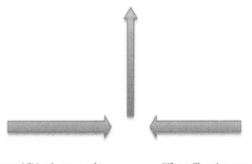

What capabilities do you need to Make this happen?   What will get in your way?

Website references:

http://www.mesadelsolnm.com/

http://www.stapletondenver.com/

Experience Economy, B. Joseph Pine II and James H. Gilmore. Harvard Business Review, 1999.

They described the experience economy as the next economy following the agrarian economy, the industrial economy, and the most recent service economy. Pine and Gilmore argue that businesses must orchestrate memorable events for their customers, and that memory itself becomes the product - the "experience". More advanced experience businesses can begin charging for the value of the "transformation" that an experience offers, e.g. as education offerings might do if they were able to participate in the value that is created by the educated individual. This, they argue, is a natural progression in the value added by the business over and above its inputs. Within the hospitality management academic programs in the US and Europe, Experience Economy is often shortened to Exponomy, and is of increasing focus.

 ® The **9E®** process

The 9E® process is evolutionary and transformational in nature – it is a journey for the rest of your life. Through a facilitated and structured process that raises your awareness of what you already know, you will become more satisfied with, engaged in, and fulfilled by the life you choose to live.

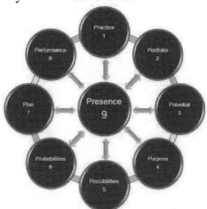

This program supports an evolutionary progression to deepening levels of satisfaction, engagement and fulfillment along with the corresponding expansion of presence. The desired outcome of the

9E process is peacefulness, which can be described as sustained fulfillment. The intent of peacefulness is to be in a state of present moment awareness where you can experience calmness and serenity, as well as being centered and grounded.

For your understanding, below is a short summary of the 9 elements.

1. Practice (foundation and understanding)
2. Portfolio (assessment work)
3. Potential (grounded in strengths, etc)
4. Purpose (definition and declaration)
5. Possibilities (form that purpose can take)
6. Probabilities (expectations, possibility analysis)
7. Plan (phased priorities over time)
8. Performance (sustained energy flow)
9. Presence (personal power and engagement)

Another way to view the 9 elements is by the internal and external nature of this work. The first four elements are data heavy and focused internally on becoming aware of who you are. With the definition of your purpose in element 4 you reach the tipping point in element 5 of the range of possibilities open for you in the external world. The remaining four elements are focused externally on aligning your behavior with who you are.

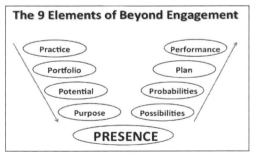

Practiced and proven over twenty years and hundreds of clients, these 9 Elements, each one worked separately and in order, are the engine, the fuel, the vehicle itself that will carry you to a more purposeful and prosperous life.

Practice: In Practice, you establish a foundation for the 9E work through a practice of self-care, determining your readiness and willingness to engage successfully in the 9E process, and becoming aware of the foundational basis from which you live your life. The outcome of the Practice element is expansion of awareness to modify your behavior to get the results that will best serve you. From "I don't know I don't know", to "I know I don't know", to "I know I know". You will gain an understanding of how your values, guiding principles, patterns, habits, standards, and boundaries influence your present behavior, choices and decisions. Through this iterative process you will understand how powerful discernment of these items can be and be ready to transition to the next element.

Portfolio: Bring all of your historical test and assessment results together with some new and leading-edge assessment devices for a fresh and surprising look at your life's work.

Potential: A series of innovative and reflective exercises will help you discover the vitality and truth that lies in the intersection between what you do best, and what you most love to do.

Purpose: Use the knowledge you gained in the previous three elements to arrive at a concrete, written statement that expresses the essence of who you are and how you can best manifest that purpose in the working world.

Possibilities: Use a number of carefully crafted exercises to discover the myriad ways you can bring your Purpose actively into your life. In this element you will stretch your mind, abandon limiting thoughts and beliefs, and use your muse to explore the exciting and infinite field of possibilities.

Probabilities: You'll be guided to conduct a time-tested cost-benefit analysis that will help you clarify how best to bring your purpose into being. In this analysis, you'll be asked to use both logic and intuition to evaluate the data, review trade-offs, and make choices. Measurable costs in dollars and time will be compared along a continuum of categories to help you determine next steps. This element helps you build a solid bridge to the final three elements.

Plan: Construct a detailed set of tasks with a timeline for their completion. These will be value-added, purposeful actions leading you to the manifestation of our deepest intention. This is the vehicle that will lead you out of inertia and into momentum. The plan you create will make it possible for you to "go where you are invited."

Performance: Practice aligning your actions with the results you've gathered, using value-added techniques. This element is about managing your energy. As you move into the final element, it is critical that you are in good condition - physically, emotionally, mentally, and spiritually.

Presence: Cultivate gratitude and self-honesty, and learn to establish boundaries so you can live more fully in the present. This will bring a heightened level of understanding about how you show up in the world; how to stand in your own power. Presence is the evolution of potential aligned to passion.

To learn more about 9E® go to: http://9eglobal.com/

Epilogue Resources

This is the edge of our universe. This is where we operate. There are a couple articles you should read as background and some websites. We are particularly fond of TED type presentations because we think that's where the communication process is going. Best way to stay current here is to follow us on Facebook, twitter and the website.

Happy futuring!

Read

Moonshots for Management, Gary Hamel et. al., Harvard Business Review, February 2009.

In May 2008, a group of management scholars and senior executives worked to define an agenda for management during the next 100 years. What drew them together was a set of shared beliefs about the importance of management and a sense of urgency about reinventing it for a new era. Topping the list is the imperative of extending management's responsibilities beyond just creating shareholder value. To do so will require both reconstructing the field's philosophical foundations so that work serves a higher purpose and fully embedding the ideas of community and citizenship into organizations.

TED Talks

Lesley Hazleton

There exists a video including Lesley's thoughts about Koran, which is supposed to be recorded at October 2010. "Lesley Hazleton sat down one day to read the Koran. And what she found -- as a non-Muslim, a self-identified "tourist" in the Islamic holy book -- wasn't what she expected. With serious scholarship and warm humor, Hazleton shares the grace, flexibility and mystery she found, in this myth-debunking talk.

http://blog.ted.com/2011/02/15/uncertainty-touches-the-best-of-what-is-human-in-us-qa-with-lesley-hazleton/

William Easterly

Economic success-among individuals, firms, products and countries-is often unexpected and unpredicted. William Easterly will draw on insights from Nobel laureate Friedrich Hayek to explain why prediction is difficult, success is rare and failure is common; the advantages of decentralized decision making to discover what works best in the market and in public policy; and the need to rely on dispersed and local knowledge, rather than government planning, for poor countries to achieve growth.

http://www.youtube.com/watch?v=0fBQyNiWOuU&NR=1

see also

http://www.youtube.com/watch?v=iaybmA_pQ30

Websites

http://www.dailykos.com/story/2011/05/17/975936/-Participative-Models:Progressive-Scenario-Planning?via=spotlight

http://www.theworldcafe.com/

http://integrallife.com/learn/overview/essential-introduction-integral-approach

http://mul.org/2011/04/beyond-the-surface-focus-fully-on-jobs/

http://www.globalfuturist.com/more-on-the-extreme-future.html

http://www.davinciinstitute.com/

http://www.stratfor.com/

http://www.comm-design.net

http://www.futureworkingtogether.com

Presentations

Workforce development for the 21st Century

www.nga.org/Files/pdf/1004EDUINSTITUTEVANHORN.PDF

http://www.youtube.com/watch?v=BltRufe5kkI

[1] Themes are derived from 'The Seven Spiritual Laws of Success" Deepak Chopra (1994) New World: San Rafael, CA.

[2] Social Networks and Marital Interaction, PhD Dissertation, C. Grantham, Univ. of Maryland, 1980.
[3] Consumer Evolution: Nine Effective Strategies to Drive Business Growth, Grantham and Carr (2002), John Wiley and sons, New York

[4] This information regarding the changing attitudes of workers has been adapted, with permission, from Interim Technology, Inc. in 2005. Data updated in 2009. Source data can be viewed at http://www.spherion.com/EW_Study/about.html.
[5] Bureau of Labor Statistics, Monthly Labor Review • January 2012
[6] A note of thanks to Dave Bayless of Evergreen Innovations Partners for helping me understand the importance of the difference in these concepts. To Chris Hoy, one of my mentors who said I had to explore this topic. Dr. Bill Arnold for his communications insight and my venture partners Terry Musch and Norma Owen who tolerate my aimless musings.
[7] Thomas Meyer, Chief European Economist of Deutsche Bank, *Economist* April 25, 2009, p. 74.

[8] Grantham, C. (1993), The Digital Workplace, New York: Van Nostrand-Reinhold.
[9] Todd Wilbur, A Theory of Everything.
[10] Excerpted from "The Future of Work", C. Grantham (2000) McGraw-Hill with permission from author.
[11] http://en.wikipedia.org/wiki/Sociology_of_emotions
[12] Herman Trend Alert: HR Responds to the Economy and Labor Market (Part 2) December 22, 2010
[13] http://en.wikipedia.org/wiki/Leadership_development#cite_note-1
[14] http://www.ccl.org/leadership/index.aspx
[15] Daft, R.L. and Lengel, R.H. (2000) *Fusion Leadership*, Barrett-Koehler: San Francisco.
[16] *System failure Why governments must learn to think differently* Second edition, Jake Chapman. Demos: UK (2004)
[17] Hofstede, G. (1997), *Culture and Organizations: Software of the Mind*, New York: McGraw-Hill.

[18] Miller, R., (et. al.)(2009) *The Commercial Real Estate Revolution: Nine Transforming Keys to Lowering Costs, Cutting Waste, and Driving Change in a Broken Industry.* New York, NY: John Wiley.

[19] Grantham, C. (2011), "Tai Chi Chin and Leadership", Vital Force Journal, Vol. 28 (2), May.

[20] http://www.frogrecruitment.co.nz/Your+Career/Future+Job+Titles.html

[21] I dismiss Avant guard entertainers from my definition because I do not believe they are truly "transformational." Experiential? Yes, but not transformational in the purest sense.

[22] http://www.huffingtonpost.com/2011/09/04/the-best-paying-jobs-of-t_n_948405.html

[23] Florida, R (2002), The Creative Class.
[24] http://eicolab.com.au/2008/08/29/from-knowledge-worker-to-conceptual-worker/
[25] http://pewresearch.org/millennials/
[26] http://flsaovertimelaw.com/2010/04/03/growth-of-unpaid-internships-may-be-illegal-ny-times-reports/
[27] http://www.pewinternet.org/Reports/2011/Social-Networking-Sites.aspx
[28] http://www.strategy-business.com/article/11110?gko=64e54

[29] Barford, I.N. and Hester, P.T. (2011) *Analysis of Generation Y Workforce Motivation Using Multiattribute Utility Theory,* Defense Acquisition University, Washington, DC.

[30] http://www.sag.org/

[31] http://www.gartner.com/research/fellows/asset_126360_1176.jsp

[32] http://en.wikipedia.org/wiki/Self-organization
[33] http://www.nationaljournal.com/njonline/no_20100225_3691.php
[34] http://en.wikipedia.org/wiki/Sustainability
[35] http://online.wsj.com/article/SB122445963016248615.html
[36] Strauss, W. and N. Howe, (1997), The Fourth Turning, Broadway Books: New York.
[37] Lautman, Mark (2011), When the Boomers Bail: A Community Economic Survival Guide, CE Associates: Albequerque, NM.

[38] 'Up skilling' is a technical governemnt term meaning to increase basic skill levles AND add new ones such as colloboration, communication

and career track management.

[39] Sheilagh Ogilvie, "Guilds, efficiency, and social capital: evidence from German proto-industry," *Economic History Review,* May 2004, Vol. 57 Issue 2, pp 286-333

[40] http://blog.sloconference.com/categories/263/artisans-of-thought.aspx

[41] http://en.wikipedia.org/wiki/Guild

[42] Whang, Sang-Min (2003) "Youth culture in online game worlds: Emergence of cyber lifestyles in Korean society" in 15th Biennial Association of Asian Social Science Research Councils released by UNESCO Bangkok, see section 16.

[43]
http://mars.acnet.wnec.edu/~grempel/courses/wc1/lectures/24guilds.html

[44] Thomas W. Malone, Robert Laubacher and Michael S. Scott Morton (2003) Inventing the Organizations of the 21st Century, MIT Press, Boston.

[45] : Kind thanks to my spirit guides for their observations and comments: Rex Miller, Terry Musch and Barry Tuchfeld.
[46] http://www.thefutureofwork.net/what_book.html
[47] Matthew Fox, "The Reinvention of Work"
http://www.matthewfox.org/sys-tmpl/door/
[48] May we suggest
http://www.amazon.com/gp/product/0385497911/103-6053708-7783037?v=glance&n=283155
[49] Peter Berger and Thomas Luckman, (1966) "The Social Construction of Reality : A Treatise in the Sociology of Knowledge"
[50] Joseph Campbell, "Hero with a Thousand Faces"
Http://en.wikipedia.org/wiki/The_Hero_With_a_Thousand_Faces

[51] http://nooventures.edublogs.org/2007-04-12-the-limits-to-the-complexity-of-social-systems-by-duane-elgin-and-robert-a-bushnell/
[52] Grantham, C. and J. Carr (2001), *Consumer Evolution,* New York: J. Wiley and Sons
[53] The Sevenfold Work comes from the ideas of John Bennett, The Sevenfold Work, Coombe Springs Press, 1979 and is part of larger metaphysical work.

Made in the USA
San Bernardino, CA
26 October 2013